Journeys Through Life Book 5

A True Story

One Text Away

A Doctor's Indecent Proposal

Tammy Horvath

TYH Publications

ISBN: 979-8-9895279-4-6 (Paperback)

ISBN: 979-8-9895279-6-0 (eBook)

First edition published 2024.

Printed in the United States of America

TYH Publications

117 Forest Street, Sidman, PA 15955

CONTENTS

1. THE STARTING LINE

Picture this: I walk into the hotel, and a tall, gorgeous man greets me with a hug, lifting me off my feet and swinging me around in a circle before handing me the most beautiful bouquet of white roses, my favorite flower. Then Dr. Carter kisses me and grabs my hand, pulling me through the hall into the elevator. Many candles light the hotel room. He pulls me to the balcony, where another bouquet of roses is on a table under the starry sky. After he pulls out my chair, I sit. The doctor leans in and kisses me before taking his seat and opening a bottle of wine. After handing me a glass, he makes a toast. "To your beauty." He knows rosé is my favorite wine as he lifts the lid off one of my favorite meals—sauteed colored peppers with filet mignon cooked to juicy perfection. He smiles as I eat. Emotion overtakes me as I contemplate my next move, and tears brim in my eyes.

· ♥ · ♥ · ♥ · ♥ · ♥ ·

My struggles with self-doubt and that temptation threatened to derail me when I thought about meeting the doctor because I felt unworthy of my husband's love. So when Dr. Carter looked at me and then propositioned me, I knew I wanted all he offered. I didn't care about the price I would pay, the loss I would suffer, and the loneliness in the end when he went back to his wife. Like an addicted gambler, I only thought about putting it all in and betting on the win. So what if I lost everything I ever loved? It would be worth it to feel worthy of love. Or so I thought. It was a battle waged within, a struggle against the shadows of doubt and insecurity. Yet amidst the chaos and racket of conflicting desires, I heard the gentle whisper of God's voice—a voice calling me home, calling me to surrender all that I was to the embrace of divine love. But would I listen?

2. How Many Opinions Are Enough?

At the water company, when it came time for my husband Mike's Commercial Driver's License renewal, he had to have a physical from the water company's doctor. After his appointment, my husband of over twenty years and the love of my life rang me. "Doc gave me some disturbing news at my visit. He is concerned about a problem. I don't think it's a problem that needs further attention because my specialist is already treating the issue with ongoing medication. He said there was nothing to worry about as long as I continued to take the prescription. But my CDL doctor doesn't feel that way."

Mike had been seeing this specialist for several years, and the doctor routinely tested him to ensure he was healthy. So Mike shrugged off the CDL doctor and went back to work.

"But two hours later, my phone again rang," Mike said. "The CDL doctor took a deep breath before he said 'I insist you see someone about this problem even though I know you don't think it's a problem. I've seen other patients with the same issues, and they ended up needing major surgery.' I agreed it wouldn't hurt to get a second opinion from another specialist," Mike said. "The secretary squeezed me in, and I have an appointment next week."

"I'm going with you." I said a quick prayer and asked God to let Mike be OK.

The office was efficient, and a thin, attractive man slightly taller than me walked into the room five minutes early. His dark hair was short and wavy; it blended perfectly with his tanned skin and contrasted with his meticulously ironed, long, white lab coat.

He introduced himself as Dr. Carter and smiled; I struggled to suppress my attraction to him as I stared. A few minutes later, I had to look at the white-tiled floor to stop myself from staring at that finely chiseled face of Adonis. He typed the information Mike gave him into the computer and reviewed Mike's chart. When I finally looked up, Dr. Carter's bright smile greeted me, revealing his perfectly white teeth. Did Mike notice how gorgeous he was? More importantly, did Mike notice I noticed?

The doctor examined Mike. "Your problem is fairly common. Many people are born like that."

Mike asked, "Is it something you can check? My CDL doctor insists I don't ignore it. He has me concerned."

Dr. Carter described the potential problem in great detail in terms both Mike and I understood. He showed us pictures on his computer of a person without any issues, then pictures of what could happen if a problem develops, at which point surgery would be needed.

"Is there any way you can make sure that won't happen to me, Doc?"

"A straightforward procedure can be done at the hospital to ensure everything is OK."

"Can you explain the procedure? Is it dangerous?" I asked.

The doctor pulled up a three-minute video and watched it with us. The video made us very comfortable, and the doctor's confidence that it was a simple procedure caused Mike to ask if he could schedule it as soon as possible.

"I'll schedule it to put you and your wife's mind at ease since I can see she's worried. I've done this many times, and it should only take thirty minutes, but you will have to be given anesthesia. Does that sound good?"

"Yes, that's fine. Thanks."

The doctor turned his dark, piercing eyes on me, and I held my breath as he asked, "Does that sound good to you, Tammy?"

I cleared my throat and stuttered, "Gr-Gr-Great!" before glancing at my flip-flops before he could read my mind. Looking back up, I added, "I've already lost my first husband to a car accident, and then my son was murdered when he was only nineteen, so I don't need to lose anyone else."

"I'm so sorry."

"Thank you. Would you like a copy of the book I've written about it?"

"Sure. Thanks."

I handed him a copy of my first book and a bookmark, which I always carried.

"Your picture is beautiful."

My face turned beet red since a close-up of my face took up the entire book cover.

Mike asked about a picture on the desk next to the computer. In it, an attractive woman was standing next to the doctor.

"That's my fiancée. She lives in another state with her family since she's in college."

"She's gorgeous," Mike said.

I wondered why the handsome doctor wasn't already married, because he appeared to be around forty. Then I thought that maybe they just had a long engagement.

Dr. Carter buzzed the front desk, and when he finished entering a few notes into his computer, he turned to Mike. "You're all set. Your appointment is next Friday at eight in the morning. I'm assuming you can drive him, Tammy?"

"Yes. No problem."

Doc smiled at me. "And how are you doing? Do you mind if I get your vitals to ensure everything is well with you?"

"Um, OK." I felt myself blush at the attention.

My heart raced as he put his stethoscope on my chest and held his head close to mine. I closed my eyes and breathed in his musk and vanilla scent. I needed to get a hold of myself. If he felt my heart racing because of his closeness, he didn't say anything as he moved his stethoscope onto my back.

His breath was warm on my neck as he said, "Take a few deep breaths for me."

I could have sworn he just sniffed my hair. Maybe my imagination was getting the best of me.

When he finished, he said, "You're perfect."

Coughing, I thought about what he meant by that comment.

I was just there to keep Mike company and to be there if we needed to decide about scheduling surgery. I did not have an appointment, so the doctor checking my vitals was odd, but we thought little about it as we left the office.

Mike had gone to Dr. Carter for a second opinion during that first visit. We both liked the doctor so much that Mike left his specialist to see Dr. Carter in the future instead. Mike also suggested I schedule an appointment with him to be safe with any health issues since we like to cycle vigorously and occasionally mountain bike. Dr. Carter was brilliant, and we trusted him implicitly.

3. Attracted to Tall, Dark, and Handsome Men

Mike got up early on the day of his procedure, and we arrived at the hospital with plenty of time to spare. I heard Dr. Carter's melodic voice from down the hall as all the nurses laughed at something he said. "Good morning. Are you ready to get prepped?" Dr. Carter asked Mike.

"Yes, I'm ready," Mike said with a smile.

"And how are you, Tammy?" His smile reached his eyes as he looked at me. I must have looked concerned because he said, "Don't worry. Everything will be fine, and I can confirm this for you within the hour. Let me show you to the waiting room."

I kissed Mike goodbye and told him I loved him before following the gorgeous doctor out of the room, where Mike was changing into a hospital gown.

"Tammy, here, take my wallet." I ran back and grabbed the wallet before catching up to the doctor as he hit the buzzer to open the door for us.

In the waiting room, Dr. Carter showed me the TV screen with a list of numbers. "When number seventy-five changes to 'surgery,' you'll know I'm working on him. It will change to 'recovery' as soon as I finish, and then I'll talk to you. There's juice and soda in the fridge. Help yourself. There are also snacks and fruit. Take anything you want."

I watched his back as he left the room and thought about the lucky woman who would marry him. Twenty minutes later, Mike's number changed, so I started reading my Kindle while I drank a glass of orange juice followed by an apple juice. When I returned from the restroom, the doctor entered the room and sat beside me in the soft gray chair. He turned his body toward me, and his leg rubbed against mine as we talked quietly. My thoughts again went to the lucky woman he would call his one day. I knew I should have been thinking about Mike, not the doctor, but I had difficulty controlling my impure thoughts.

"I'm not going to remember what you tell me since I have PTSD. Do you mind if I record it?"

"Not at all."

"I'll just use the video because I don't know how else to record on my iPhone."

"There's an audio button. Here, let me show you." As I handed him my phone, his hand bumped mine. Shivers ran up my spine as it felt like I'd been shocked. That was the first time he had touched me. On the day I was in the office, only his stethoscope touched me and his chin when it had bumped the back of my head, and that alone had caused my pulse to race. My heart was pounding so hard today that I felt he would ask me to quiet it. "I can't find the recording button, so use the video. I don't mind." He returned the phone, and I was careful not to touch him that time. After I started recording, he said that everything went well and that Mike shouldn't have any problems in the future, along with much more detailed information, which I can't remember. I wondered why I'd allowed the devil to tempt me that way.

I was so relieved that Mike didn't have any problems that I wanted to hug the doctor to thank him for the excellent news. But I didn't think it would be appropriate, especially since other people were in the room. "Thanks, Doc."

He put his arm around me and said, "Let's get you back to your husband," as he led me out the door. Shivers ran through my body from his touch as we walked a hundred feet to Mike's room.

Mike was awake, but Dr. Carter had gone to check on another patient when he left me, so I played the video for Mike. The two nurses at the station ten feet from us jumped when they heard the doctor's voice since they'd just seen him walk down the hall. They gave me strange looks when they realized the voice was coming from my phone. "It's OK. He said I could record him." They smiled and were relieved, although I'm not sure why they cared. We overheard them and others talking about Dr. Carter possibly moving away; therefore, he'd be changing offices. It would be too far for Mike and me to drive to see him.

Mike and I looked at each other. "It's always that way when you find a great doctor," Mike said. "I know I'll be bummed if he moves."

"Me too," I said.

I heard the doctor laugh the whole way down the hall. He was always so cheerful. It was infectious. He brought joy to everyone around him and put them at ease. I heard him coming before he entered the room. He explained everything to Mike and told him what to watch for in the future. If the two things he said never happened, Mike wouldn't ever need another test like that again. What a relief!

"Are you leaving the office, Doc?" I asked.

"I might take a job closer to my fiancée."

"We'll miss you," Mike and I both said simultaneously.

"When are you leaving?" I asked.

"I don't know that I am. It hasn't been decided yet."

Mike got dressed, and we said our goodbyes. Dr. Carter hugged me before I left the room, but I couldn't keep my mind out of the gutter because his cologne was on my hair for the rest of the day. Why had God made someone that handsome? Not that Mike wasn't because he is a blue-eyed, blond, attractive angel who loves God and loves me. It was too bad that I'd always been attracted to the tall, dark, and handsome type ever since I'd met my first husband, who'd towered over me with dark brown hair and eyes to match. But he was a devil and had made my life a living hell, unlike Mike, who treated me like a princess—and I loved him for it. So why I was allowing my mind to have those impure thoughts was beyond me.

Three days after we visited with Doctor Carter, my phone dinged. I read the text.

Thanks again for this book! I will read it soon! Nathan.

"Mike, I just got a strange text."

"From who?"

"I've no idea."

Mike read the text. "I don't know anyone named Nathan."

Four hours later, my phone dinged again.

> Nathan Xanderon Carter is what I meant, your new doctor.

"You'll never guess who that text was from?"

"Who?"

My eyes widened as I looked at Mike. "Our new doctor."

"How'd he get your number?" Mike asked.

"I guess from the office file. Or did I give him one of our business cards? I've no idea."

Dr. Carter started texting me nonstop and talked to both Mike and me that way. The first texts only discussed health issues, mainly about my sleep habits, even though by then we were both patients. I read all of those texts to Mike. I didn't want any secrets. Mike and I both felt a strong connection to our new friend, and we even invited him to our home for cornhole tournaments, a game in which you throw bean bags into holes, and the team that wins receives a cash prize. But the doctor always had to work or was on call.

He mentioned getting together sometime in the text.

> I need you both; you're a package deal.

He was still texting both Mike and me, even though it was only through my phone.

Everything was completely normal on our next office visit. The three of us joked around and enjoyed each other's company. Mike and I always make people laugh wherever we go—we play off each other well and crack jokes.

Dr. Carter, who we were both now calling Nathan, Nate for short, wasn't like anyone I'd ever met; he was full of life. His soul-searching eyes made all the ladies swoon over him. Those eyes could melt ice. People wanted to please him and went out of their way to talk to him.

A week later, we were still texting. I reminded Nathan that the secretary hadn't received the files from my previous doctor, and he'd texted back that he'd get them to review—we texted inconsequential things like that.

Everything took a turn when the texts came late into the night. Mike always went to bed early, but sometimes I couldn't fall asleep. Nate and I texted for hours and talked about everything and anything. I never thought there was anything wrong with texting him, and I always told Mike what we discussed the following morning. But I was naive. I always have been. So much so that when I first met Mike and men hit on me right in front of him, Mike would point it out, and I always said, "Nooo."

After our last appointment with the doctor, he left the office, got married, planned to start a family immediately, and took a new job. I refused to see his replacement, but Mike did. Nate hadn't texted me in months, but that would change in the future.

4. A Nightmare for Christmas

Have you ever had a health scare? Fear consumed me, and sweat covered my skin as God allowed the devil to convince me I'd die from breast cancer when a lump doubled in size in just a year. I'd have been happy to have the lump removed immediately. But that's not how doctors or health care works. Instead, they poked me and sent me for test after test, all while telling me it was nothing to worry about while I got bill after bill and owed thousands of dollars. Then they would probably tell me I was dying anyway. So why not just cut the lump out and be done with it? But no, that was not to be.

I knew worrying would do more harm than good. After all, I only have one body.

Nothing exciting had happened in the last several months, but that was all about to change. While making an itinerary for our upcoming trip to the Turks and Caicos, my gynecologist called to schedule an ultrasound to recheck a few tender breast lumps. My mom, sister, and I all have fibrocystic breasts, and it's necessary to take precautions since my grandma had to have her breast removed because they found cancer. The checkup was essential because my breasts were tender. No, that's not accurate. They were downright sore. The dreary weather matched my mood on the way to my appointment, and the radio blasted "Feel Like Makin' Love" by Bad Company—I wanted to shout at Paul Rodgers to shut up. But instead, I said a quick prayer that everything would be OK. Little did I know God was already lining up people to help me through my upcoming ordeal.

Sitting in a hospital gown in the icy room, I watched the technician with her brown hair in a tight ponytail review all my papers from my previous test results. Then she gelled my breasts and pushed on my painful lumps while staring at the screen and hitting buttons on her computer. She hadn't said anything after instructing me to lie on the bed. That was until she pressed harder on my left breast and let out a loud "Hmm."

"What? Do you see something?"

"Does this lump bother you?" she asked, pushing on the spot in question.

"Ouch. Yes. That's one reason I'm here." I pointed to a spot on my other breast. "And this lump hurts too."

After capturing several more images, she said in a no-nonsense way, "The doctor will call you with the results."

Her comment had scared me, but I was glad the thirty minutes of torture were over.

·♥·♥·♥·♥·♥·

Nicole from my gynecologist's office called the next day. "The ultrasound again found spots on both breasts; you need to go for a mammogram right away."

"I can't bear to go through that again; I had pain for four months after my last mammogram."

Nicole cleared her throat. "Will you at least meet with the doctor to discuss it further?"

"What's the point if I refuse to get a mammogram?"

"You have nodules and lesions. They may be calcification. But when they clump, they can hide masses behind them."

"Never again!" Tears poured down my cheeks as I repeated myself. "I will never get another mammogram as long as I live. I don't care if I die of cancer. The pain is unbearable. Let me call you back."

I was in my early fifties. My once problematic son was now in heaven, and Mike's three kids had long ago moved out of our house. They were all doing well and had jobs they loved, and the youngest was happily married. Mike and I were blessed with a joyful marriage and steadily cruised through life—no speed tickets here. I knew Mike loved me with all his heart, and I felt the same. But these breast lumps brought life to a screeching halt.

I knew what was coming next—a biopsy. I'm not a doctor and don't know much, but I did a lot of research. Before my appointment, I had searched for a facility that offered elastography ultrasounds. But none of the local offices provided them for breasts. This advanced radiology can reduce the number of biopsies needed because it can validate the absence of fibrosis using imaging two hundred times faster than conventional ultrasounds. It checks whether the tissue is firm because cancerous tissue typically tends to be stiffer. I was willing to drive long distances, but our local doctor said his office only did them on livers, and he didn't know where I could get one.

When I called Nicole back, she said, "Please reconsider getting the mammogram."

I explained to her it had even hurt to wear a bra after my last mammogram and that the pain had started as soon as my right breast was compressed. I had told the technician to stop, but she said the doctor needed accurate pictures. Tears poured as the machine gripped my breast tighter and tighter until I could take it no more. I screamed and made her stop. After I finally got control of myself, she turned my body and inserted my other breast. My mind screamed at her, but nothing came out of my mouth. I was so terrified that I could not speak. The machine again squeezed tighter and tighter until I cried out in pain, begging the technician again to stop. But the technician didn't seem to care, so I grabbed my breast and tried to pry it from the machine, which ended up causing more pain and bruises.

"I guarantee our employees here won't do that if you tell them to stop," Nicole said.

"No!"

"Then the doctor suggests you get an ultrasound-guided core biopsy."

There it was. I knew it was coming, but that didn't make it easier to hear. *Why was I dealing with this nightmare right before Christmas?* I buried my face in my hands. Finally, I asked, "What does that involve?"

"The doctor will use the ultrasound to guide a needle to grab a sample of the suspicious lump. A biopsy is the only way you can be sure that the abnormality isn't cancer."

"I'll think about it. The secretary at your office tried to get me to have a biopsy last year too. But I refused because many tumors go away on their own, and nearly everyone has cells that *can* contain cancer or pre-cancer. But you don't always get cancer. And I'm willing to risk knowing that I *can* get cancer."

Nicole was the secretary for my gynecologist, Dr. Menser. However, the doctor who suggested an ultrasound was a different doctor because Dr. Menser had left the day I had my pelvic exam, one week before my life turned upside down at that dreaded ultrasound. I had trusted Dr. Menser, but I didn't know anything about the reputation of this new doctor. So I saw a breast specialist that I'd seen in the past when I had pain.

·♥·♥·♥·♥·♥·

Dr. Stefanick was gorgeous, and her friendly manner reminded me of my mom. She shook her head with concern when I said I didn't want a biopsy. Then she held my hand while she addressed all my questions. "Tammy, this needs to be your first priority."

"Fine. Against my better judgment, I'll get the biopsy." I trusted her and knew she cared for me.

"Great. Someone will be in touch."

Jill, the secretary at Dr. Stefanick's office, called. "Advanced Imaging will call you to make arrangements for the biopsy. Call me back if you don't hear from them in a few days."

Scheduling called, and Karissa said, "You're scheduled for a left breast biopsy, but what about the other lump next to it?"

"I only thought I needed one biopsy because the lump doubled. It's now seven by seven millimeters."

"The doctor actually recommends three biopsies."

"No!"

"I'll call you after I confirm this."

My mind raced. If those suspicious lumps didn't kill me, stress would. I remember someone telling me that the needle used in the biopsy could cause a malignant cell to separate from a tumor, which then allowed it to spread to the rest of the body, but my doctor said that core needles don't cause cells to spread. I wasn't sure what I believed.

My hand shook as I listened to Karissa. "I have you scheduled for three biopsies—two on your left breast and one on your right. We'll see you soon. You can eat and drink normally, but please quit taking blood thinners."

·♥·♥·♥·♥·♥·

My sister Jamie went with me to my appointment, where I learned I needed both breasts examined via an ultrasound since the original machine at the breast center in Windber was a decade old.

"Many biopsies get canceled because they're unnecessary," Karissa said.

"That's great news. I hope I'm blessed with not needing one."

The technician gelled both breasts and captured several images. Finally, Doctor Wolfel looked at the results live as the technician scanned my breasts for a third time. "You have what we call 'busy' breasts. I can't justifiably do a biopsy on one lump over the numerous other lumps. It's impossible to pick out just one."

"OK." Karissa was kind enough to bring Jamie into the room, and I was glad to have her support since all the information was going over my head.

Jamie asked, "What do you suggest, Doc?" My sister had told me earlier that she trusted this doctor.

We called Mike after the appointment. Jamie explained, "The doctor didn't do the biopsies because the original ultrasound machine was twelve years old. They did more ultrasounds, but the doctor can't justify carrying out a biopsy on one lump over the other. She thinks they're all cysts, but she wants to be sure. She ordered an MRI to see if anything 'lights up' or if everything is normal."

"I guess that's great news," Mike said.

"It is. There's nothing to worry about. She thinks they're cysts."

I spoke up. "Says you. I'm the one that has to go into that tunnel. I'm severely claustrophobic. And the bill will be $1,500 since I haven't met my deductible yet this year."

"Yes, but it will be worth knowing they're just cysts, so you can quit worrying." Mike said goodbye and hung up as my sister and I headed to our favorite Mexican restaurant to celebrate the good news.

The waiting began. More stress. Again.

My chicken nachos covered in salsa, sour cream, and peppers were delicious. "I don't like the idea of getting radiation."

"What are you talking about?" Jamie asked.

"With the MRI. Isn't it like an x-ray?" I dipped another chip into the delicious salsa as I stared at my sister.

Jamie put her fork down and took a drink before answering. "No. MRI means magnetic resonance imaging."

"Yeah, but there's radiation in the machine."

Jamie laughed at me.

"What?" I asked.

"The machine uses magnets and radio waves. There isn't any radiation."

"Oh." Feeling stupid, I shoved another bite of food into my mouth. I tried to take care of my health as much as possible. I avoided radiation at the airports and asked for a pat down instead of going through the scanners. Recently, I quit doing that because it took too long. My thoughts were that I had to die somehow.

After lunch, I went home to wait for my phone to ring. One week later, I was scheduled for my MRI.

·♥·♥·♥·♥·♥·

I curled my hair on Christmas morning so I would look gorgeous for pictures I'd refused to have taken for the last several years because of weight gain. It took almost an hour, and I didn't like how my hair turned out. But it would have to do.

Mike walked into the bathroom as I sprayed hairspray to hold my blond hair in place.

"Do you like my hair?" I asked.

Mike looked at me and laughed. "Umm. I think you should jump in the shower and start over."

Picking up my phone, I tried to unlock it to get a picture. "It won't unlock, and it wants me to enter the passcode."

"See, even your phone doesn't recognize you." Mike laughed harder as he looked at my face, now turning red because I couldn't control my laughter.

"You hate it."

"I told you it was fine the way it was," Mike said. He always likes my hair straight. We had a good laugh, and I made a video to savor our moment for the future.

·❤·❤·❤·❤·❤·

But gone was the laughter when, the following day, I remembered my MRI was in a few days. My sister, Mike, and my mom had all offered to go with me, and Jamie had told me to request anxiety medicine to calm my nerves. But I hadn't asked, and I planned to go alone. The lady who scheduled my visit said that I would be face-down with my breasts poking through holes in the scanner bed. She told me I would be able to see the floor, but she hadn't been in the machine herself, so I planned to keep my eyes closed before entering the room. It would be better not to take any chances.

On the day of my scheduled visit, I woke early, showered, and dressed. The kind technician inserted something into my arm so they could add the dye when the time came. I held onto her shoulders and followed her into the room with my eyes closed. After climbing the steps, I faced down and positioned my breasts so they hung through the holes.

Another technician entered the room. "I'm going to put earplugs on you because the machine is loud." She pushed them into both of my ears.

"The left one won't stay in," I said as I squeezed it, trying to get it deeper into my ear.

"Do you want headphones?"

"Sure."

After covering my ears with the headphones, she explained what would happen. "You'll be in the machine for twenty minutes. You won't feel anything, but it'll be loud. Do you want a call button in case you need us?"

"Um. Sure. I guess," I said, obviously very nervous. She handed me an oval-shaped object that felt like it was made of plastic. My hands rubbed over it, but I didn't feel a button. Oh well, I didn't plan to use it anyway. I could figure it out if I needed it.

"The dye won't enter you until we're almost done."

I wasn't sure which tech said that, but it didn't matter. My pastor suggested I pray while in the long tube-like machine. He thought it might distract my nerves from what was happening, since he was also claustrophobic. So, I concentrated on God as life around me faded away.

5. Death Knocks at My Door

The bed moved, and after the machine turned on, I heard a whirring sound like air moving around me, which pulled me out of my prayer. My back was hot after about five minutes, but I wasn't sure why. The banging began almost immediately, mixed with constant clicking sounds. My mind raced as I pictured telling Mike, my parents, and my sister that I had cancer. I could see myself going through the rest of my life without a breast or two, just like Grandma. My hair would probably fall out from chemotherapy—the beautiful long blond hair that had just finally grown back after having cut it all off two years ago when it had started falling out from COVID-19. I needed to take my mind off the procedure, or I'd hit the call button before my results were processed. Every year, I write a poem, "'Twas the Night Before Christmas," for my blog, so I started working on it so I wouldn't think about my surroundings. The poem usually shared my forgiveness toward the man who murdered my son. His name is Tyrone.

> 'Twas the night before Christmas; I
> longed for the past,

> When my family was whole and my joy
> still held fast.

The stockings were hung by the chimney
with care,

But I ached for my son...

Bang—more whirring. Click. Click. Click. It sounded like the machine was falling apart. I panicked. *Should I press the call button?* I needed to occupy my mind if I was going to get through this. OK, where was I?

'Twas the night before Christmas; I
longed for the past,

When my family was whole and my joy
still held fast.

The stockings were hung by the chimney
with care,

But I ached for my son...

Hmm. I got it.

... who was no longer there.

Wow! My back was on fire. I wondered if there were lights on the machine heating it. If not, what caused the hot sensation? Then it sounded like a saw had turned on. My mind raced. My arms had fallen asleep in the last ten minutes, and I fought to make them move while trying to keep my body still as I caressed the call button, wishing to push it and make all this madness end. The noise didn't stop, and I knew I had to control my thoughts.

'Twas the night before Christmas; I longed for the past,

When my family was whole and my joy still held fast.

The stockings were hung by the chimney with care,

But I ached for my son, who was no longer there.

I nestled with Mike in the warmth of our bed,

While a vision of heaven danced round in my head.

I soared up above, through the clouds, and took flight,

And I know I met Jesus in heaven that
night.

Hmm. What next? I know.

A high wall of jasper, a huge pearly gate;

My eyes opened wide when I saw my
son's fate;

Luke's home, now eternal...

An announcement came from a speaker on the machine. I think the tech
said, "We're inserting the dye." But I wasn't sure until I felt pain in my arm.
Then I knew. I prayed for it to be over quickly. My chest ached, and I wasn't
sure why. *Focus on your poem.*

My back ached. My neck hurt. When would this be over? The scan must
have been almost finished since the lady with long blond hair said she would
only release the dye when they were nearly done. But there was more clicking.
Click. Bang. Click. I told myself to concentrate on the poem.

A high wall of jasper, a huge pearly gate;

My eyes opened wide when I saw my
son's fate;

Luke's home, now eternal, beyond all
my dreams,

God's peace and the throne where his
holy light beams.

An ocean of crystal and lanterns of gold,

A rainbow of emerald; such sights to be-
hold!

The thunder, the lightning, the fanfares
galore;

Such wonders I'd never imagined before.

Suddenly, I thought I felt the bed move. But I didn't dare open my eyes. "You're finished. Be careful getting up."

As I lifted my stiff body, I pushed where my breasts had been resting in the holes. "Don't lean on that," the technician said as she helped me sit upright. She grasped my elbow to steady me as I climbed down the three foot-high steps.

"Oh no!" She grabbed my arm. "Did your arm look like that before?"

"Like what?" I asked.

She called the other tech back into the room saying, "It looks like saline leaked into her arm."

The shorter lady ran into the still darkened room as we stood near the light from the hall. She flipped on the light switch. "Let me see." After staring at my now puffy, strange-looking arm, she said, "Let me see your other arm." She grabbed my arm and pulled my hand in the air before I could respond.

"It does look puffy," I said, comparing my arms.

"Take her to the paramedic and ask him to give her an ice pack," she said to her coworker.

But before leaving the room, I looked my fear in the face as I stared at the MRI machine. I figured I was safe since I was done and wouldn't need another one for the foreseeable future. Oh, how wrong I was.

Back in the front office, the paramedic was busy with another patient, so an assistant got me an ice pack. "That's for later. Bend it to release the cold and tape it to your arm." She walked over to the cupboard and returned with another thick pad. "This one is heat. I'll tape it to your arm. Use whichever makes you feel better—heat or cold."

I felt dizzy as I wobbled out of the office. I couldn't breathe and had to sit in a chair in the waiting room before returning to my car to call my husband. "Mike, I finished. But I can't breathe, and I'm dizzy. I feel like I'm having a heart attack." *Was death knocking at my door?*

"Maybe it's the dye. Call an ambulance or go back inside if it's that bad."

"No. I don't want to bother anyone. Maybe I just need to eat."

"I'm leaving work. Stay where you are, and I'll come pick you up."

"No, Mike. I don't want to be a bother. I'll grab some food and probably feel better after eating. Maybe it's just low blood sugar."

We hung up. I tried to pray but couldn't form the words. *Tammy, why did you wait so long to get these lumps checked? This could have been done a year ago.* I drove two blocks to Burger King and used my coupon to get chicken fries before driving the ten minutes home. I felt slightly better after eating. But I was still exhausted, so I napped until Mike got home.

"I'm worried about you, Tammy. You're still dizzy, your chest hurts, and you can't breathe. That sounds like an allergic reaction. Ask your sister."

They only use a small amount of dye, which shouldn't cause any problems.

Jamie's reply should have put me at ease, but it didn't.

·♥·♥·♥·♥·♥·

The next morning, nothing had changed. Perhaps it was a pulled muscle since much of my body weight had rested on my chest during the MRI. But that didn't explain the dizziness. I suffered for the next several days as I not so patiently waited for the doctor to call with my results. It would probably take almost a week since it was a holiday weekend.

·♥·♥·♥·♥·♥·

We had the Horvath family Christmas party the following weekend since getting everyone together on the actual holiday was impossible. Over fifty people came to our house for a meal. There were games and gift exchanges, and we did the traditional ornament exchange where everyone made enough homemade tree ornaments to give the others, and each received one back. I never took part in the exchange after the first time when I'd made cute, colorful plastic canvas designs and put hooks on the back of them. Someone, not going to mention any names here, said that my ornaments were stupid. So that moment remains locked in my past, along with my hurt feelings.

·♥·♥·♥·♥·♥·

Finally, my doctor's assistant, Jill, called. "The radiologist wants to complete an MRI-guided biopsy because they found a six-millimeter irregular enhanced mass in the upper outer quadrant. There isn't anything else suspicious that you need to worry about. Can I call in the request?"

My mind raced as I remembered looking at the machine that had wrapped me in a tight embrace. How could I face it again? Why had I glanced at it? I was desperate to avoid confronting the monster that filled my nightmares with clanks and heated my body, making me feel like I would burst into flames at any second. I didn't think I could go back into the tunnel. The only tunnel I wanted to enter was the one in movies where someone was transitioning from Earth to heaven. Why didn't God take me now instead of putting me through this? This was it. I was going to die from cancer. Mike would cry for me, but he'd eventually find a new wife while I joined my son in heaven.

It had taken me forever to agree to the ultrasound biopsy, and then I had fought again about not wanting an MRI. Finally, I had done as I was asked. Now they were trying to kill me by making me face my worst fear—again! "Can't they just remove the lump? I don't want a biopsy."

"Hold on while I check."

"Hi, Tammy. It's Doctor Stefanick. They can't remove the lump until they know if it's cancerous. There's only a 20 percent chance that it's cancer, and until then, there's nothing we can do."

"Who would remove the lump if I can get my insurance to approve it?"

"A surgeon would remove it. But the lump can't be seen with an ultrasound, so you need to let them do the MRI-guided biopsy. It's the only way to be sure. You need to trust that I know what I'm doing. I'll order the biopsy now with your permission."

I hung up and thought about how many things in this life were out of my control. Did I have cancer, and if so, was I going to die? If I wanted a lump cut out, why couldn't I have someone remove that lump instead of poking me with a needle? I was tempted to drive to Mexico and pay a doctor cash to cut the lump out of my breast. Instead, I gave the doctor permission, and she said scheduling would contact me with the date. But I was still uncertain if I'd actually do it. I was concerned about spreading cancer through my body if the mass was cancer. In my opinion, you can't just go poking holes into cancerous masses and expect them to sit still until they can be removed—this very rarely happens, but you must understand where I'm coming from. Rare things happen to me—I've lost a husband and my only child. But what matters is that I sometimes look at what *can* happen, not what will probably happen. As much as I didn't want to get the biopsy, lots of family members and friends had opinions about what I should do:

"Well, if it doubled in size over a year, there's something not 100 percent."

"Tammy, I know this is scary, but everyone who cares about you is likely to be afraid of what will happen to you if you don't get that biopsy. And there's nothing they can do about their legit fears because you make the decision. The number of people who die from MRI-related issues is probably minuscule compared to how many die from lack of treatment. I'd suggest weighing this out before the Lord and trusting the advice of those who most care about you, as well as medical professionals. Perhaps God wants you to trust him with this fear too."

"You must get the biopsy. It's more likely nothing, but if it is, you must accept treatment. You have God's work to do. You're reaching people through Luke's story—don't let it all be in vain."

After those comments, I felt I didn't have a choice, so I scheduled the biopsy. Someone was supposed to call me so I could prepay, but no one did, so I called them. After several calls to the doctor's office, the imaging center, and the UPMC health plan, I still had no idea what it would cost. No one could tell me, and I'd wasted two hours trying to find out. The only thing I knew for sure was that I didn't need preapproval. Well, who cared about that? I just needed to know how much money this would cost. Along with all that stress, I had to wait for three weeks. I was sick of waiting and wanted to move on with life and put this behind me.

6. An Unexpected Proposal

As time passed while waiting to get the biopsy, my life took another unexpected turn. One day, Nathan texted. It had been over four months since he'd moved and our last text. I had no idea what had caused him to reach out, but I mentioned my upcoming trip to Australia when he asked what was happening in my life. That's when Nate said I was gorgeous and suggested we meet in Australia. Our texts got a little out of hand when the doctor started talking about sex. He'd begun to talk about sex months before, but it was in the aspect of him suggesting lovemaking with Mike before bed would help with sleep problems, so I didn't think too negatively about his comments. Well, maybe a little, if I'm being honest. So even though I felt uncomfortable now, I replied to his questions, stating things that should have been only for my husband's ears. But when it came to Nathan, I couldn't think clearly. My fingers typed my likes and dislikes into my phone as my brain willed them to stop typing. But I didn't. Why, I will never know. I had so many regrets as I stayed awake most of the night, worried about the Pandora's Box I had just opened. Was it too late to close it? Had the damage been done?

My bottomless faith in God and my relationship with him were powerful. They had been ever since Luke died. But I am also human. So when Dr. Carter suggested having an affair, I'll admit it tempted me. I felt like a tornado had swept me off my feet. The blood in my veins sizzled every time I thought of him. My husband was always with me when we'd met at his office since we had scheduled our appointments together as we did with all our doctors, so

I'd done nothing wrong—until now. But I longed for Nate's attention. And now that I had it, what would I do?

Nate said he'd fantasized about sleeping with me while watching a video I'd sent him from something I'd posted on social media. Until that moment, I'd felt innocent. Well, almost. Now, we were on a whole new level. The proper thing to do would have been to stop texting and come clean with my husband, the love of my life, about what had happened. Then I should have blocked all contact with the doctor to stop my lustful fantasies that were starting to consume me.

I reprimanded myself for my thoughts, biting my bottom lip as I scoffed at the thought of acting on impulse. I wanted to meet him, and I don't even know where the fantasies came from, but they were there—my body wrapped in the arms of Adonis. From that night on, my life took a turn for the worse because I knew I'd already sinned according to Matthew 5:27–28: "You have heard that it was said, 'You shall not commit adultery.' But I tell you that anyone who looks at a woman lustfully has already committed adultery with her in his heart." My faith was deep, but my body wasn't listening to my brain. Therefore, in God's eyes, I'd already sinned. But sleeping with the gorgeous Dr. Carter was on a whole other level. I needed to remember that even though my body was weak, God was stronger.

Ever since I'd met Mike, my life had been perfect. Both of our spouses had cheated on us in our younger years, and we knew what it felt like to be betrayed. I also had once cheated on my first husband before he died in a fiery car crash. But that was different. My first husband, Tony, cheated on me during our entire relationship. And when I confronted him, he continued to cheat. It had really hurt. I'm not making excuses for myself because what I did was wrong. And even though my marriage to Mike felt like a dream come true, that didn't stop me from thinking the grass was greener on the other side. Did I want a new life? Is the old saying true: Once a cheater, always a cheater? A quick Google search said statistics say that just because you cheated once doesn't mean you will cheat again. But if you have cheated three times, you likely will have another affair. Hmm.

Mike and I had been married for more than two decades. We could finish each other's sentences, but the spark was gone. I tried every day to make

Mike happy. I took it too far, attempting to please him by buying everything he hinted at wanting. Even if he looked at something, I bought it for him. Sometimes, he didn't even like it; he'd just been curious about the item. And such was our monotonous life. The only thing adventurous that we did was travel. Even *that* had become boring because I wanted to rent a car and explore the places we visited, but Mike was content sitting on the beach every day. Yes, every single day. Sigh. At home, we occasionally went out to eat. We never went bowling, to the movies, or out to watch bands anymore like we used to do in our younger days. Life was stale. And so was our marriage. It didn't mean we didn't love each other. We did. As I said before, I know Mike loves me with all his heart. And I love him too.

So why was I allowing the devil to tempt me this way? Tears threatened to spill as I thought about how God had given humans free will when he created them. He mostly lets us do whatever we choose, but if we go against his will for our lives, there are consequences to pay. So why would I consider doing something that would ruin my perfect, dull life? But that was precisely the problem. I craved excitement, just like a drug addict craves their next fix—or so I'm told. I wanted to feel alive again. Full of life. I wanted a reason to get out of bed every day. I wanted someone to look at me the way Mike used to. Like I was the hottest woman on the planet. I needed to find that confidence that I once had in my appearance.

Yes, my husband still found me attractive, and he let me know it by occasionally tapping my behind. OK, you're right, he still did that on a daily basis. But the intense lovemaking was missing, along with the cherished hours we used to spend cuddling. We used to take long drives and talk about the future. We used to want the same things. But now, Mike didn't like to sit on a plane for more than six hours, and I still wanted to see the world. So Mike had been allowing me to do just that without him. But that was OK. I recently went to Canada and spent more than two weeks with a Christian couple I'd met online. The husband, Michael Copple, is a fabulous writer and has published many books. His wife, Elfriede, is a firecracker. She was just what I needed to put joy back into my life. We visited six national parks in Canada while I stayed with them, and I had a fabulous adventure—I even got to see the northern lights. That night brought back those precious memories of how God healed me two months after my son had been murdered when I saw the dancing queen on a solo trip to Iceland.

My son Luke had been my world for nineteen years, and he was gone in a second when Tyrone McDuffie shot a single bullet that instantly killed him—the only thing I had left from my first marriage to Luke's dad, Tony. That marriage, too, had ended in disaster when Tony decided he wouldn't be a perfect dad and went on an inevitable suicide mission, leaving me a single mom of my one-year-old son at the young age of twenty-eight. That marriage had been full of life. An action-packed, miserable life. Every day was an adventure, as Tony cheated on me and partied like he was a teenager even though he was in his thirties. Nothing was dull about life with Tony. I'd been miserable as he caroused around with young teenyboppers breaking the law by dating and being intimate with girls not yet eighteen. But I digress; back to the story. My story. My life. My perfect life. And how I was thinking about ruining it.

I texted back.

> What are you thinking?

Nate replied.

> I want to see you in Australia.

> Are you bringing your wife?

> Do you want me to?

> Yes, I want you to. I'd love to meet her.

I clicked send and prayed that I could meet both of them in Australia since I was nervous about going alone.

> My wife is too busy with school and her job. It would just be me.

What should I say?

I'd really hoped that he'd be able to talk his wife into this once-in-a-lifetime trip, which I was sure they'd enjoy. I sent one last text to Nate.

> I'll never cheat on my husband.

He replied.

> I'll never cheat on my wife.

But *he* had suggested meeting, and I didn't think then, and I don't think now that it was in a platonic sense. Constant thoughts of taking him up on his offer had taken over my thinking since that last text. But for what? To ruin my marriage? But the temptation was real.

Mike was the only good thing left in my life since losing Luke, other than God. And I knew God wasn't too happy with me. I felt like history was repeating itself. But, as I said, God gives us free will. So, I was the one who needed to ask God to get me through this and to shut the devil down with all of his temptations. Satan worked overtime, making it look like life could be great if I cheated on Mike. Sure, I could have the time of my life for one night and then spend the rest of my life alone, without Mike, crying myself to sleep every night because I'd been stupid enough to act on an impulse.

Ruining my life was just one text away.

And I was so tempted. But only time would tell what would happen.

·♥·♥·♥·♥·♥·

I was in a tailspin. Mike knew something was wrong when I said, "Mike, I have a problem. It's bad. But I can't tell you what the problem is."

"You can always tell me your problems." Mike pulled me into a tight embrace.

Tears poured down my face as I held back a sob so Mike wouldn't know how bad my problem actually was. "I won't tell you. But will you pray for me?"

Friends also prayed for me, but I wouldn't admit that I had thoughts of having an affair. Trying to spice up our life, I played pool with Mike. We even went bowling, but after walking into the bowling alley, we both decided it was too busy. Mike said the arthritis in his elbow would hurt for weeks if he played a game. He loved me and would do it if that's what I wanted. Instead, we left. For Christmas, I'd bought us gift certificates to an escape room. We needed to use them before they expired. We'd tried one at our time-share in Virginia, and I loved it. But Mike didn't like it, even though he was much better at it than me. He told me I could take someone else with his ticket. Spicing up our marriage wasn't working because it takes two to tango, and Mike wouldn't take dance lessons either.

But Mike gave me the freedom I craved. He was letting me take a three-week solo trip to Australia, where I'd meet other authors and readers I'd gotten to know on Facebook. It would be an epic trip, and I was so excited, although I wished Mike would go with me. But I was already dragging him to Hawaii on a fourteen-hour flight. Back in 2014, I booked a trip for Mike and myself to Australia, but then my son got arrested, so Mike said, "You need to cancel the trip. We can't be halfway around the world while Luke acts this way." So I canceled my dream trip.

All my life, I'd known I wanted to travel. After all, that's why Mike and I owned five time-shares. But Mike didn't want to go anywhere cold or take long flights. He even agreed to let me return to Iceland for a week with a local family I knew well since we'd worked together in real estate, and I was also taking a trip to Alaska with my long-lost childhood friend. I was definitely looking forward to my upcoming trips.

That was my new life. Things would be better. Or so I thought. Deep inside, I knew I had feelings for someone other than my husband. I hadn't physically cheated, but it was definitely an affair of the heart.

7. Making Bad Choices

After Luke's murder, I had turned to alcohol to cope. My dad was an alcoholic and had been all his life. So drinking was dangerous for me because there was a higher risk that I'd permanently become addicted too. A few years after Luke's death, I quit drinking. But recently, I'd turned to the bottle again.

As a Christian, I knew that if I surrendered my life to God, he would fix everything. So, I put my body, mind, and soul into God's hands and started living my new life. The life God intended me to live. Mike and I spent day one of my new life with Mike's family, playing board games. We had a blast, other than when his sister brought up politics, which is never suitable to discuss with Mike's family since they are all headstrong. Not that I wasn't. The night finished well without any arguments because neither Mike nor I responded to the political comments.

·♥·♥·♥·♥·♥·

Day two was spent with me exercising so I could try to take off the stubborn weight that I'd gained since Luke died in 2017. When Mike first started dating me, I'd been skinny and attractive. He still found me alluring, but he longed for me to have the gorgeous body I used to have, and he knew all the additional weight I'd put on was not healthy. I knew this because Mike often shared his thoughts with me. We weren't afraid of hurting each other's feelings, and from the time we said our marriage vows, we agreed to be honest with each other. I know what you're thinking. As women age, their bodies and hormones change, which opens a world of unique problems: belly fat increases, and the pounds pile on each day. Most people don't look bad; they just *think* they do. But that was not my case. I wasn't simply trying to look like I had when I was thirty. Several people told me it was vital to take the weight off, since it would eventually lead to other health problems. Mike's body still looked the same as when I'd met him. Actually, he looked better since he was thinner. But I was the complete opposite. My entire middle section looked like a balloon as my belly and butt popped. But taking weight off is a lot harder than putting it on. After I exercised, I used our massage chair to relax, then I played a game of pool by myself. I vowed to get better at the game and everything else in life. This was my new life, the life where I would not cheat on my husband, so it had to be better.

With the seventy-pound weight gain, I had become more depressed. I already struggled with PTSD and depression since Luke's death, but every time the scale went up, my spirits went down. As I worked from home as a full-time writer, I hadn't worn makeup in years, except when Mike and I went to church every week. I vowed to look better for my husband, so every day, I decorated my face in an attempt to look beautiful in my fat body.

Growing up, I had learned in my Presbyterian Church that the husband was supposed to be the head of the family. He was to lead me in prayer and Bible readings. But Mike had never done that, and I longed for that because whenever we prayed for something meaningful together, it was me doing it. I wasn't very good at it; I had only prayed out loud about twenty times. As far as I knew, Mike had only prayed out loud twice. I understood his fear, but I wanted a Godly husband and the bond other Christians had by worshipping together at home. I truly believe in Proverbs 22:6, "A family that prays together stays together."

That night, I had a dream about Luke. He told me he loved me and that he always had my back. I missed him terribly. He was the one person I could always talk to who never judged me. Oh, how I missed those days. In the dream, soldiers were taking control of the streets, just like the devil was trying to control me. Luke and I were trying to make it through the woods to his friend's house so we could relocate to the safety of the country, just like I was trying to keep my marriage safe. The other part of the reason I dreamed that is that I feel my freedom will eventually be taken away even though I live in America, the land of the free, and I believe that will happen sooner rather than later. You heard it here first. It was a terrifying dream, but I truly expect someday that we will all be under the control of a one-world government. And I don't want to be alive when that happens. I pray every day for God to end the world. Then, I will get to join my son in heaven. But God knows what he's doing, and the Bible says that the world will not end if there is one person left who will accept him as their Savior, so I'm patiently waiting. But there are signs that the end is near. War is breaking out, earthquakes are increasing, famine is spreading, and Christians are being persecuted. But that's for another book, so let's get back to my story. No matter what I dream, I love spending time with my son. And since I rarely remember my dreams, it's a blessing to wake up and recall them. But I usually forget soon after if I don't write them down. I guess this is a problem everyone has as they get old. If only Luke had given me advice about what to do about my marriage in that dream.

Since losing Luke, I've never really shared how bad my struggles are. Recently, I've opened up to Mike about how I have to trick my brain so that I can fall asleep at night. This is embarrassing, but I'm going to tell you how bad my life really is. And I'm sure you will think I'm crazy afterward. Every night, I cradle my belly and think back to when Luke was still inside me before I gave birth. It's the only way I feel like my son is still with me and not dead. I know—I sound psychotic. But I do what I must do to continue living and be there for my family and friends. It's more challenging during the day because I know Luke is dead, and I miss him so much that I suffer from broken heart syndrome. Every morning when I put on my deodorant, I talk to Luke's picture hanging inside my medicine cabinet. Even though I know he's happy in heaven, it doesn't stop the pain I feel from missing him, and I also always talk to him when I need something from his bedroom. Someday, we'll meet again. I wish God would make that today.

·♥·♥·♥·♥·♥·

That night, Nate texted.

> Happy New Year.

As I replied, I thought about his athletic body and sun-kissed skin.

> Happy New Year. Hope you had fun.

> I did. Hope you did. Resolution?

Oh boy. Did he really want to know my resolution? Should I tell him? I didn't want him to think of me as unattractive. Well, I was always an open book.

> Lose weight. But I haven't been successful at that the last ten times I tried.

> LOL. You look great. Just do things slowly. Nothing radical.

Of course, he thought I looked great. He hadn't seen me in more than five months, and I'd been depressed over the holidays and had packed on a few more pounds.

> I swear I'm diabetic or pre-diabetic. I get sick every time I diet.

Staring at my phone, I waited for his reply.

> Hmm. Get your blood work checked.

> I was a stick before Luke's murder, but I constantly worked to stay that way.

We stopped texting, and I went to sleep.

·♥·♥·♥·♥·♥·

The following day, my thoughts lingered on Luke. I probably had dreamed about my son, but I didn't remember.

A phone call took my mind off Luke. Mike and I had played in a pool league several years ago, and now a new season was about to start. But they were short a few people to complete their team. Bobby asked if Mike and I wanted to join. We'd had a lot of fun the last time we were in the league. Well, we had a blast until we didn't. During one game, my competitor's husband was coaching her. Mind you, the rules permitted this. We were each allowed one coach of our choosing. And I needed all the help I could get. My problem was that I usually missed the mark whenever my coach told me to do something—the ball rarely went into the hole. My coach was usually my husband, although I tried to get anyone to help me except him because he made me nervous, and I felt like I let him down every time. On that occasion, the lady's husband stood behind her, telling her to move her pool cue left, then right. Then it happened. He grabbed her stick and moved it himself. She took the shot and sunk the eight ball, winning the game. To say I was furious was an understatement. I stomped over to the boss and complained. "That was illegal. The woman's husband may as well have taken the shot himself."

My husband kept his mouth shut. My dad was in the other room at the bar. An older gentleman, Henry, who had been great friends with my first husband, came to my defense. He walked up to the husband and pushed on his chest. "Tell your wife she needs to forfeit the game."

"No. It's fair."

"It's not. You moved her cue. That's not allowed," Henry yelled. Fists were ready to fly as the men stood their ground and took a fighting position. They shouted at each other. Judging by their red faces, their blood pressure was probably through the roof. I knew this wouldn't end well. When a wrestling match started, several men jumped in to break up the fight. Had they not, someone would soon have gotten hurt. It didn't end there. Even though the husband was forced into the next room to cool down, the men shouted back and forth.

Trying to defuse the situation, I hugged Henry and told him, "Let it go. It's OK," although I was still furious. But it wasn't worth fighting over. If they were comfortable cheating, fine, let them. I found out later, and still to this day, that neither the wife nor the husband think they did anything wrong. And the husband still hates Henry. What had I done?

Bobby awaited our answer. I needed to text him soon. *Did Nathan play pool?* Now, where had that thought come from?

Mike said, "We can join the league if you want to."

"I don't want to be on the team with certain people, and I don't want to go through what I did last time."

"Well, you'll eventually have to play both of them," Mike said.

"Bobby said it's on a weeknight, which means you'll get less sleep for work."

"Yes, but it's only one night a week for ten weeks. I can handle it if that's what you want."

"Mike, you already fall asleep every night at eight o'clock, and this won't end until ten or eleven."

Mike and I both do things to make each other happy because that's what you do to have a wonderful marriage. I texted Bobby and told him we wouldn't be joining the league, partly because Mike was already tired every day, and I was terrified that something more was happening with his health. I didn't want to say anything because I didn't want to make it come true. The other reason I didn't join was that I stank at playing pool. Maybe I could find something I was good at someday.

8. A STORM BREWS

After showering in the morning, our Amazon Echo Dot interrupted my music. "The US National Weather Service has issued a severe winter weather advisory for Sidman. It will be in effect until ten p.m." OK. No problem. Since I only left the house on the weekend to go to church, I didn't need notifications to tell me if it wasn't safe to head outside. There was already a full-blown whiteout when I peered out the window. Mike had said that we could get up to five inches of snow later, and I was sure he wasn't looking forward to shoveling the sidewalks for our house and our vast apartment building next door, which consisted of five rentals. He also needed to plow the three driveways that belonged to the house and apartments. But he wanted the rent money we received because he hoped to retire someday, and social security didn't look promising since the government kept saying it would be out of money soon. So we were stuck if he ever wanted to retire.

I took full advantage of the weather when the snow let up around dinner-time. "Mike, I want to have a date night."

"OK. What do you want to do because we can't drive anywhere?" Mike had been out earlier for his job because of a power outage at one of the Highland Sewer and Water pump stations. His work truck had acted up, and the four-wheel-drive feature hadn't engaged. The man from the electric company ended up pulling Mike's truck up the hill on the unplowed road in Cresson. Mike had said that they had a foot of snow there. I wished I could have seen it.

"I want to build a snowman. It's been at least forty years since I've done that."

"Hmm. That's an interesting choice."

"I need to go through Luke's winter clothing and find a pair of gloves. Mine are all dress gloves; I don't want to get them dirty. They aren't made for playing in the snow."

"I have gloves you can wear."

The sun had already set, and the sky was free of stars, but the moon was partially visible. Six inches of powdery snow glistened next to our garage's light, and I reveled in seeing it without any footprints. It was eerily quiet and blustery, causing snow to hit my face. There was another storm in the forecast, but we had a few hours. We had enough light after turning on the porch light, so I tried to make a ball out of the snow. I yelled to Mike, who was in the garage, "Mike, what am I doing wrong? It keeps falling apart."

"Just roll the ball around the yard until it's the size you want."

I tried again. Success. So much for date night, though, because Mike was still in the garage instead of helping me. Finally, he came out.

"This is painful on my legs, Mike." I stood up and took a break to stare at Mike as he started a snowball, and then I finished mine, almost crashing into him as we both rolled our balls around in the snow until they were a perfect size.

Mine was too heavy to carry, so Mike moved it to the edge of the driveway, where I wanted the snowman on display for others to enjoy as they drove past.

"Can you get me two pieces of coal from the basement for the eyes, Mike?" We had a coal furnace and included the heat in the cost of our tenants' rental units, so that was perfect. While Mike got the coal, I rolled the head, making a flat edge to set on top of the two other balls. Then I grabbed the carrot and scarf I'd put on the kitchen counter.

Mike handed me several pieces of coal.

"Mike, can you get a drill or screwdriver? The carrot won't go through the icy snow." Mike rescued me again while I went to the woods to grab branches for the arms.

"Umm. Tammy? These arms are three feet long."

"OK. Well, the pickings were slim." I'd grabbed some brown sticks that were weeds instead of branches, but I couldn't make them shorter since they were too thin at the ends.

Just then, our neighbor stopped the car as she drove by. "It looks like you're having fun."

"We are. Want to join us?"

"No. I'm good. But you need a carrot for the nose."

"It's there, but you can't see it in the dark."

As the neighbor left, Mike went into the garage to get a hat. I took the opportunity to capture a picture of Mike while he placed it on the snowman's head. That activity was meant to make Mike and me close like we'd been in the past, especially while biking over the summer, but it was too cold for that now.

"Mike, take a picture of me with Mr. Snow Man."

Mike laughed as I handed him my phone.

"Why did you put a stick between the bottom and middle?" I said as I pulled on the stick.

"I didn't."

"Oh, never mind. It's the arm."

Mike laughed. "You impaled him."

"Oh boy. I had to keep pushing the sticks into the belly to shorten the arms." I pulled that stick back out of his side a little so he wasn't impaled. Now, his arm was longer than ever. "He doesn't look half bad with his stylish green and burgundy scarf and black hat. But he needs a mouth."

Mike shoved extra pieces of coal onto the face, but it didn't look right, so I curved a twig and used that instead. I would do anything to get my marriage back on track and find the excitement we once had—even if it took building a snowman in my fifties.

·♥·♥·♥·♥·♥·

Later, in the comfort of my bed, I thought about how I had forgotten to put buttons on. Maybe Mike and I could build a whole family this week since the temperature would remain cold, and it called for more snow.

I texted Nathan a picture of me with Mr. Snow Man.
He replied.

> Love it.

> Haha. He has three-foot arms.

> Basketball snowman.

Even though it was funny, I didn't reply because I needed to get a grip on our relationship—the relationship we shouldn't have. The relationship I kept pursuing. Why couldn't I stop thinking about Nate? Would I ruin my life? How far would I go? Deep inside, I knew I didn't want to lose our friendship. But I still wanted more. Maybe I should give up and divorce Mike. I was hopelessly in lust.

·♥·♥·♥·♥·♥·

A storm blew in like no other had in a long time. Temperatures were below freezing, and at six a.m., the blizzard began. Mike had a horrible time driving his truck to work because he couldn't see the road. He called two hours later. "My work truck is stuck in a ditch. The office is sending someone to pull it out."

"Are you hurt?"

"No. But the snow is over my bumper."

"Did you get your four-wheel-drive working?" I asked.

"Yes. It works. But this snow is deep. It calls for rain this afternoon, and the roads are already a mess. The plows can't keep up with clearing the snow."

"Mike, WJAC TV says we're only supposed to get up to eight inches before the rain begins."

"There's over a foot of snow here. I need to go so I can shovel around my tires before help arrives."

"OK. I love you, Mike. Be careful."

The plow finally came down our road, and the snow along the edge was two feet high. But when the rain hit, the snow melted as the temperature rose into the forties. That evening, it took Mike over two hours to plow our three driveways and another hour to shovel the sidewalks. I was sad because Mr. Snow Man looked depressed as he tilted forward from the high winds and rain. He reminded me of myself, and the dark, dreary weather only added to my sadness. Mr. Snow Man eventually lost his head, and I cried.

Hoping it would distract me from my sadness, I grabbed a puzzle depicting fifteen different Christmas cookies. I didn't expect Mike to help, but after he'd eaten dinner, he started putting pieces together.

"I didn't think you liked puzzles," I said.

"Now that you took a break from writing, I'm enjoying spending time with you."

"Oh!"

Every time we sat down, it was harder to see the pieces. We continued to work silently until our backs hurt from standing over the puzzle for an hour.

"Want to play pool?" Mike asked.

"Sure."

In our basement, Mike rubbed my neck and shoulders as I racked the balls for him to break. We had a fabulous time, and I got better at pool every time we played. But the better I got, the better Mike became too. We played six games, and we each won three. My mind raced as Mike showered before bed. How was I even considering cheating on this incredible man?

9. Past Mistakes

A wistful smile came and disappeared just as quickly as I imagined seeing the beautiful, white-toothed smile on Nathan's handsome face—just the thought of never seeing him upset me. I was addicted to the idea of being with him as much as I was addicted to overeating. Why was I thinking of him when I should be thinking of my husband and our happy life together? Once, when I sold real estate, I developed feelings for one of the other agents. I knew I was weak, so I quit my job because I knew it was risky being alone with the man several days a week since we were both on the same shift, answering phones. The other two people who were on our team never showed up. I didn't tell Mike why I'd quit that job until years later. And when I told him, he agreed that I'd made the right decision.

It hadn't taken long to finish the Christmas cookie puzzle, and then we moved on to a puzzle called Selfies, which had four adorable kittens in Christmas hats sitting among presents, snowmen, and yellow lanterns under a blue sky. Time flew by as we rubbed our aching backs while finding piece after piece. We worked on that one past our bedtime and finished it in under six hours before capturing a photo so we would remember that night.

As Mike kissed me goodnight, he said, "The temperatures will only be in the teens over the next week. I assume you aren't going out?"

"No, I don't have plans," I replied. "Luke's birthday is coming up, and I want to do an escape room with the certificates I bought to celebrate, even though Luke is in heaven." I snuggled close to Mike.

He wrapped his arm around me as I rested my head on his shoulder. "Sure. If that's what you want, but you need to find someone to go with us who knows what they're doing." Mike pulled the covers tighter around me, knowing I was always cold at night.

·♥·♥·♥·♥·♥·

I slept peacefully, but the next day was far from peaceful as I spent hours arguing with Conemaugh Hospital's billing department because they hadn't charged me enough for my MRI. I'd repeatedly mentioned that my deductible was $1,500, but they insisted the estimate was only $500. You probably wonder why I would be upset because they charged me less. It's because when you prepay your bill, Conemaugh offers a 20 percent discount. And that is a lot of money that I could have saved. After much debate, I finally talked to Alycia in the billing department, and she offered me a discount if I paid my $1,000 balance. In the worst-case scenario, I'd call and ask for a refund.

Knowing I needed to be distracted from the upcoming MRI-guided biopsy, Mike suggested we enter the cornhole tournament at the Beaverdale Legion that weekend. "You always have so much fun when you play."

I shook my head. "I never win, and it costs money I'd rather spend traveling."

"We're going. You'll have fun. I know it." Mike brushed my hair behind my ear, kissed my cheek, and then pulled me into a tight embrace.

Even though we hadn't texted for weeks, my thoughts drifted to Nate as I imagined running away from my life. There wouldn't be any health worries in that life because I'd ignore all the testing and warnings in my body. The lump in my breasts wouldn't hurt, and my stress would dissolve. Life would be perfect. We could take a vacation to Tahiti and sit on the beach with a drink in our hands as we watched a golden sunset over the gorgeous turquoise water. The sound of the waves lapping on the shore would remove all my cares. If I ever wanted to see Tahiti or any other vacation destination in that part of the world, it would have to be without Mike. Oh, how I dreamed of the perfect man who would travel the world with me. But what was I thinking? Nathan had a wife, and I didn't think he was planning on leaving her. I truly loved Mike with all my heart. I felt so sinful at that moment that I wished God would strike me dead and take me to heaven, where I would sin no more. Satan had found my weakness. And I had let him by not guarding my heart more. I needed to turn to God, beg for forgiveness, and move past those terrible, impure, lustful thoughts that consumed me. Many people were hooked on watching porn, and I always wondered how they could do that to their loved ones. Was I any different? I needed to remember Psalm 32:5: "Then I acknowledged my sin to you and did not cover up my iniquity. I said, 'I will confess my transgressions to the Lord.' And you forgave the guilt of my sin."

Mike and I started another puzzle. Lang made this one, and the pieces were of high quality. And tiny. Several snowmen were under the black night sky, and colorful red and green presents were in the snow. After finishing the border, Mike and I had only found twenty pieces in three hours. Yes, three hours.

"Tammy, we should put the puzzle back in the box."

"I know. It's horrible." My back ached, and Mike saw me trying to rub it. He gave me a quick massage before picking up another puzzle piece.

"Have you ever done a puzzle this hard?" I asked.

"No. The problem is that all the pieces are the exact same shape."

Thirty white pieces were lined up in three rows on the table. To find one piece, I went through each piece, trying it where I was working. Sometimes, I thought I'd save time if I tried the piece in three places simultaneously, but that got confusing. We kept working in silence.

"Mike, do you want to listen to an audiobook?"

"You know I don't like to read."

"I know. But I just bought *Greenlights* by Matthew McConaughey, and I think you'll love it."

Mike tried several more pieces and scratched his head.

After taking a sip of my alpine berry-flavored tea, I said, "Why don't I start the book? We can always shut it off."

"Sure." I was sure Mike was hooked on the book by the end of the intro-duction. Every sentence was interesting. There was never a dull moment, and

Matthew told his story phenomenally well. His voice pulled us in, and his life, well, it was full of life—and green lights that meant he'd accomplished something, or a door had opened and blessed him. Listening to audiobooks while we did puzzles became a habit, and time always flew by. Sometimes, we'd start another puzzle just to listen to another book. It was time for bed before we knew it. Our hips, backs, and shoulders cried out in pain as we sunk into bed.

"I love you," Mike said.

"I love you too." A tear rolled onto my pillow as I already felt like I'd been unfaithful—and I had, according to Matthew 5:27–28. It all started with a thought. And I'd had a lot of them lately.

10. HEADING TO THE SALOON

My long-lost friend Mandy was finally available to hang out. I'd thought I'd lost her when I hurt her during a trip to Virginia almost two years ago. My book *Deep Inside* shares that story, so I'll summarize it here. I'd left the condo without telling anyone because I'd become suicidal after drinking wine while playing games with Mandy and her sister. It happened because they were talking to their children on FaceTime. Luke was never out of my thoughts, and I pushed myself over the edge with grief, knowing I couldn't ever see him again. Knowing I shouldn't feel that way made me upset with myself for overreacting to a normal, everyday occurrence. I thought I'd blown it and lost that dear childhood friend for good. So saying I was excited to hang out with her was putting it mildly, and knowing she'd forgiven me for my actions melted my heart.

Mandy, her husband John, and their daughter joined Mike and me for an escape room experience in Johnstown.

Mike and I were five minutes from the location when my phone rang. It was Mandy. "Where are you?"

"On our way to Johnstown."

"Aren't we doing the one at 814 Lanes and Games?"

"No. Sorry. I meant to remind you, but my mind has been so scattered with my upcoming biopsy that I forgot to text you."

Mike looked at me as we listened. "Hop on Route 56, heading west to Johnstown, and get off the first exit," Mike told Mandy on my speakerphone.

Putting the phone to my ear, I said, "It's on Clinton Street."

It was already 2:10, and we were supposed to be there at 2:15. Mandy said, "I don't think we're going to make it in time."

"Technically, it doesn't start until 2:30. So I'm sure you'll be fine."

After hanging up, Mike parked the car on a side street.

"You know there's parking across the road from the building, right?" I asked.

"Yes. Do you want me to move it?"

"No. This is fine," I said. Mike walked around the corner to locate the business as I packed up my purse after taking my keys out. "Can you throw this in the trunk? But make sure no one sees you." Luke had been murdered a few blocks from where we were, and I never had a sense of ease anytime I was in Johnstown.

Mike and I waited to cross the two-lane street, but the pedestrian light wouldn't change to permit us to cross. Mike grabbed my hand. "Come on."

"You know we're jaywalking." I stumbled as I ran to keep up. "We could get a fine."

"There isn't a car in sight."

He was right, but I didn't want a ticket if a cop came along. A sign on the building said to use the side door. We checked in with the man behind the counter. I explained our friends were on their way since they had gone to the wrong address.

"No problem. I'm Chad," the dark-haired young man said.

"Mike, can you go back outside and flag Mandy down when they drive by? I don't want to go because I didn't wear a coat, and the building is hard to spot."

"I don't know what they're driving. They just got a new car. Call her on your phone and hand it to me." After I handed him my phone, Mike left the building.

Mike, Mandy, John, and their daughter, Gianna, appeared five minutes later, wearing smiles. Mandy headed to the restroom.

"Which one are we doing?" John asked, staring into the cave-like room.

"We can do either. I was planning on doing The Saloon," I said, pointing to the room with a bar and tables. "But Bigfoot's Revenge looks cool. Chad, which one will leave first?"

"The Saloon was supposed to leave more than four months ago, so it's on its way out."

John, Mike, and I stared at each other. "How about we do The Saloon today, and if we like it, we can come back sometime and do Bigfoot since it will still be around for a while?" I said. We all agreed that was a great idea.

When Mandy came out of the bathroom, Chad gave us the instructions. "Someone has planted a bomb in The Saloon, and you have one hour to deactivate it and three clues for help if you need them. This room is ranked as hard, so you'll need them." Chad looked at the time and showed us the door we should enter before pointing to a wall in the room above the bar. "That sign shows your time and how many clues you've used. Each clue beyond the three allotted will deduct five minutes from your time."

"OK. So three clues it is." I laughed.

"It will take a few minutes to get the clock going, but you can start now," Chad said as he closed the door behind him.

Everyone scattered. After assessing the room, I shouted, "I need four digits for two locks and four letters for the other. Oh, and I need one key."

John and Gianna were behind the bar. Mike looked at a table with poker hands and chips on it. Mandy was studying a math formula written at the end of the bar. There was a piano against the back wall, and I remembered the online videos I'd studied beforehand that said to always look under tables. I'd already looked under the four in the room, so I pulled out the piano bench, planning to flip it upside down. It was then that I noticed the lid opened on the seat. "I got a key!" I yelled. I inserted the key into a lock under a table. "Here's our first clue. It's a menu." Mandy stood next to me. I stared at the menu. "A few prices are in bold," I said before leaving Mandy to look elsewhere while she studied the menu. We continued to open locked boxes as we found more codes. We now had a total of four menus. Next to them was a master key glued to the table. At least one hundred shallow holes in the table fit the bottle caps we'd gathered with our clues. A few of the boxes we'd unlocked contained even more bottle caps. Mandy used the code to fill the holes with the caps, and a pattern started to form—but we didn't know that then.

After twenty minutes, we were stuck, so we asked for a clue. Chad's typed message appeared on the screen. "Try to recycle the wooden bottles on the bar." Mike was on top of that, and a hidden message under a sliding door appeared as each bottle deposited raised the door higher, giving us our next clue. Time was ticking, and we were down to twenty minutes. Another clue told us to gather marbles, and Mandy attempted to solve the math problem while I was busy adding more bottle tops to our table with holes using the master key and menus we'd gathered. It was very time-consuming. A further clue told us to add the numbers for the marble clue. Mandy noticed her mistake. She'd missed the end where the wooden sign said to add one thousand to the total. Now we had another four-digit code. We were so close. Chad gave us a few more clues, but time ran out. He showed us the table and said we would've gotten four digits after entering the bottle caps. We needed those digits to open the wall safe to obtain a small bottle that held a number to disable the bomb. That would have given us three of the four digits. The final digit was locked in the last box. If we could have opened two more things, we would have won. So close. We'd had a blast.

Gianna said, "Let's do the other one."

"I'm willing if you guys want to," I said.

But Mandy and John had spent more than $75 on their tickets, so we decided to return to celebrate Mandy's birthday the following week. We left and headed to Fox's for dinner. I ate breadsticks, and everyone was shocked when I didn't order anything else. I said, "If I'm breaking my diet, it'll be for something I'm craving." After an hour, we said goodbye and planned to meet again to attempt to defeat Bigfoot's Revenge.

11. Was PTSD Causing Me to Withdraw?

Over the last several months, maybe years, I'd been leaving the house less and less. Not that I'd left much before. Lately, however, I'd refused to go to church. Realizing I didn't want to be around people, I'd make an excuse for why I didn't want to go with Mike. I was also lazy. And Mike was too, so he rarely complained. Even the cornhole tournament caused me stress. Since it was the middle of winter, the games were held inside. Being around so many people in one room wasn't a good idea. My son had been the same—he wouldn't go anywhere if more than a few people were present. I had several jobs before becoming a full-time writer working from home, so I don't know precisely when my problem started. I knew things were worsening, except when it came to my love for traveling—then nothing could stand in my way. The thrill of experiencing new sights and sounds ignited a surge of adrenaline, overwhelming any fear I had.

I thought that doing research might help shed some light on my issues, so I put off talking to Mike. In the past, I'd gone on solo trips only to stay in the condo for the entire trip. That was a whole week. And it didn't bother me in the least. My body would sweat anytime I dressed to leave the house. Then a panic attack set in—not a full-blown attack, I never got those—but enough to make my heart race and anxiety consume me. I also got dizzy sometimes—I think it depended on how many people were there. What's odd is that once I was around people, I was fine talking to them and didn't feel afraid—most of the time. And I love public speaking. It doesn't bother me in the least. I love standing in front of a room full of people and talking about my books and my forgiveness and love towards my son's killer. I always feel honored when someone asks me to give an update on the relationship that I'm building with Tyrone through my calls, letters, and visits to the prison, which I share in my book, *Deep Inside*. It was just the idea of actually leaving the house and getting there. Then I feared walking into the building. My friends and family loved me. Even the members of my church cared for me. So why was I afraid to see them?

I'd already told Mike that I didn't think I would go to the cornhole tournament. He didn't ask why. Maybe he knew I had issues. It wouldn't hurt to discuss it with him to get his thoughts. Dr. Wieczorek was my family doctor, but I hadn't seen him in years since I've never had health concerns that needed to be addressed by my primary care physician. The doctors I visited were the rheumatologist who treated my fibromyalgia, breast specialist, gynecologist, and Dr. Carter. Maybe my problems had something to do with fibromyalgia—I'd ask Dr. Kivits at my next appointment just to be sure it wasn't a side effect.

A quick Google search says that people with fibromyalgia may have sensory overload. The chronic condition mainly affects the central nervous system. My doctor only diagnosed me with it because I often felt like I had the flu for several days at a time. And it happened too frequently for me to have the flu. My body would ache, and I was tired, but I didn't think I had any other symptoms. Fibromyalgia is one of those labels that applies to people when much testing and bloodwork yield no results. After researching the condition, I saw I had other symptoms, like fatigue, depression, sleep problems, memory issues, and problems concentrating—maybe I actually have fibromyalgia. I assumed those symptoms were from my PTSD caused by the loss of my son. My doctor put me on a mild anti-inflammatory and said he needed to justify why he prescribed the medicine—hence the fibromyalgia diagnosis. Who he needed to justify it to was beyond me. And I didn't think to ask.

The weird thing was when I started on low-dose naltrexone, also known as LDN, it really helped. But there were many side effects; one night, I would sleep like a baby, and the next, I couldn't sleep at all. Constant headaches plagued me for the first week, but by the second week, I almost felt like a new person. My body moved like a ballet dancer flying through the air. I felt alive and free again. But then came the heartburn. I tried Tums, but they didn't help enough. Mom suggested I mix a half teaspoon of baking soda in four ounces of water. That worked great the first time I used it, but it was hit or miss after that. Still, there were many other medicines out there that caused much more severe problems, so I decided to stay on the LDN, since different treatments would require more medication to deal with the unwanted side effects.

It was getting late when Mike yelled, "Tammy, we need to leave for the tournament!"

"I don't even know if I'm going!" I replied.

Mike didn't say anything else as he continued to watch TV in the next room. Twenty minutes later, I heard him put his shoes on. I was already dressed, had my hair styled beautifully, and had my makeup on when I walked out of the bedroom five minutes later. Grabbing a bottle of rosé wine, I slid the scissors over the foil that covered the cork.

Mike walked into the room. "Here, let me do that." He unscrewed the cork as I filled my Contigo cup with ice, and then he handed me the bottle.

I poured a third of the bottle into the cup, then held the bottle up to the light and looked at it. "Hmmm." I poured a little more. "How much do you think I need?"

"That's up to you," Mike said, throwing the cork into the trash can and putting the wine opener away.

Pouring more into my cup, I looked at Mike and said, "That should do it."

Mike smiled at me. "Do you think you have enough?"

"You're right." I filled the cup to the rim before inserting a plastic sealer into the bottle. "Ready? Let's go."

"Tammy, that's a lot of wine. You got sick the last time you drank that much."

"No. When I got sick, I'd drank the entire bottle just to see *if* I could do it." I held the bottle of wine at eye level. "See? There's still one-third left."

Mike held my cup as I put on my Skechers. "Are you ready? If we don't leave now, we'll miss the signup cutoff."

"I need a coat, but I don't want to wear Luke's hoodie because I'm afraid I'll forget it at the legion, and then it will be gone forever." I'd been wearing my son's clothes so that I could feel close to him. Life was always more challenging over the holidays and in January, his birth month. "Do you care if I wear your gray coat?" I asked Mike. "It matches the yoga pants I'm wearing."

"Sure. Help yourself." Mike set the house alarm as I locked the door.

·❤·❤·❤·❤·❤·

At the legion, I joined my neighbor and played a warmup game with her daughter and future son-in-law. It started well, and I was making holes. This was going to be a good day. Mike paid our entrance fee of fifteen dollars each. There would be a cash prize for first and second place. At the last tournament, Mike, and the neighbor I was now playing with took first place. I hoped we'd recover our money this time too. Mike's nephew Josh drew names since team members were matched at random. Then Josh designated the order in which the seven teams would play. I was on team seven and didn't know my partner, Emma, who hadn't arrived yet.

Two sets of cornhole boards had been set up so that the game would move along at a faster pace. Eight people were already in the middle of their games when Emma arrived carrying her toddler. I recognized her and realized she'd brought her child to these events in the past. Concerned about the smoke getting into the child's lungs, I wished the people at the bar in the next room would quit smoking. But I didn't have control over anyone's actions but my own. Thank God I'd never started that nasty habit. When I was thirteen, my cousin Janice smoked. One day, I'd asked her to let me take a hit. She did. I'm so grateful to her for it because I coughed until my face turned red—I never tried smoking again. When I'd met Mike, he smoked. I put up with it for a few months before I finally said, "It's me or the cigarettes. You choose." You know the outcome since we've been married for twenty years. He has no regrets about the marriage or quitting smoking. In fact, he thinks smoking is a disgusting habit.

When it was finally my turn to play, I took my position and did OK, but Emma and I were playing against the best of the best. I made a few holes, which gave us points, but Emma wasn't doing well, and before I knew it, the game was over.

While busy playing cornhole, I wasn't nervous with people around. It must have been because my mind was preoccupied. Between games, I'd twirl my hair through my fingers and stand in the corner so no one would bother me.

Emma walked over to me as I took my position when it was time for our next match. It was double elimination, meaning you had to lose twice to be eliminated from the tournament. "My husband is taking over for me since I just had surgery. I thought I'd be well enough to play, but it hurt too bad."

That explained a lot. I'd had no chance of beating the last team we'd played since I was the only one making points. She should have spoken up when the previous game started, and we could have found a solution rather than throwing the game.

This game went well, and we were in the lead for most of the game. And then it happened. We went over the twenty-one points needed to win the game. When that occurs, you fall back to fifteen. It was then that the other team bolted ahead and defeated us. I was bummed because I wanted to play more, but we were kicked out of the tournament because we'd lost twice. Mike's team was still in the running and hadn't lost yet. His partner was the neighbor I'd warmed up with during our practice games. I liked her, so I stood beside her to provide moral support as I tried to give her confidence that she could hit the hole. Their game lasted for over an hour because both teams kept going over and had to fall back to fifteen points numerous times.

"I just wish this was over," Mike said. "I don't even care if we lose." He'd been called out to work for the water company the previous night when his phone had alerted him to a low chlorine level at one of the pump stations he managed. Needless to say, he was tired and cranky. In the end, they lost, and Mike was happy. I think his attitude might have made him try less.

Typically, we'd play another tournament, but there were still three games to determine the winners. "Josh, can we play another tournament after this one finishes?"

"No. This one has taken too long already."

I told Mike, and we went home to attend church that evening.

·♥·♥·♥·♥·♥·

Later that night, I got a little dizzy when I closed my eyes in bed. My MRI was a few days away. Stress was probably contributing to my dizziness. Mike and I had noticed this happening several times. I knew I needed to surrender my fear to God that he would use everything for my good, as the Bible says in Romans 8:28. But I was really struggling. Praying that night, I asked God to forgive me for drinking too much along with my other sins, which included thinking about Nate impurely. Again.

I couldn't sleep as thoughts of going back into that awful machine consumed me. Tossing and turning, I considered canceling the appointment and letting the cards fall where they may. If I died, that would be OK because I'd be with my son. But what about Mike? He'd be upset if he lost me. As would my sister, nephews, parents, in-laws, and friends. Why was life so hard? Why had God allowed the devil to tempt me with Nate's offer? Why was I still thinking about it?

12. Getting Burned

The following day, I clicked through an email to sign in for my MRI appointment. That's when I saw that an MRI can cause burn injuries. So that was why my back had been hot. The internet listed many cases where people have had first or second-degree burns. Great. Something else to worry about. One website said direct skin contact had caused the burns or possibly heat conduction. Oh my.

When I crawled out of bed for my very early appointment, I struggled to shower. I was lightheaded, or maybe I was dizzy. I don't really know the difference.

Over the sound of the water, I heard Mike pacing in the bathroom for ten minutes. He'd sit on the bathtub, then stand again, only to sit back down twenty seconds later. I saw his shadow through the shower curtain. Finally, he popped his head in the shower. "I'm leaving."

"What? Why are you leaving so early?"

"I can stay if you don't want me to leave yet." He stared at me as I put shampoo on my hair.

"Yes. Please stay. You have time." After lathering my hair, I rinsed it and used the conditioner before getting out of the shower. "I feel sick. Maybe I should cancel."

"Tammy, it's just your nerves." Mike handed me a towel. "Do you want me to drive you?"

"No. I don't want to lose money from your paycheck." After hanging the towel on the rack, I combed my hair. It was knotty, so I reached into the vanity for spray conditioner. I staggered as I almost fell over. "Oh, no!" It was then I realized I'd grabbed the wrong bottle.

Mike came into the room. "What's wrong? You used hairspray instead of conditioner, didn't you?"

"Yes. Today is a nightmare."

"You need to get your mind off your appointment." Mike started my daily devotions on my phone. After I finished the first one, he said, "I'm leaving. Call me if you decide you want me to drive you."

"There's no point, Mike. I get there, and they take me right back into the dressing room, so I won't even see you."

"I know. But call if you need me. I'm here for you," he said. "What are you most afraid of? The test or the results?"

"The test, of course. The results are in God's hands, but I have to face that machine again, and also, I'm worried the needle in my breast is going to hurt."

Mike pulled me into a tight embrace. "You got this. You'll be fine." Mike left after a last anxious look because he needed to get to work. I wondered how I would get through the day without having a meltdown. I dressed, brushed my teeth, and listened to devotions as I walked out the door for my appointment. It was freezing outside, so I was glad my car was in the warm garage. I hoped that my dizziness would stop and that I wouldn't have an accident.

·♥·♥·❤·♥·♥·

Even with my jangled nerves, I made the ten-minute drive safely and went to check in. I was five minutes late.

"Are you Tammy?" the receptionist asked.

"Yes."

She tapped on her keyboard and looked at her computer screen. "Let me get you checked in. They just called to see if you were here. I told them that maybe you went to the check-in desk down the hall."

"Yeah. Sorry about that. I've been nervous all morning and couldn't get the dizziness to stop so I could drive." I handed my driver's license and insurance card to her under the glass partition.

"Can you confirm your birthdate?"

After confirming my date of birth, she returned my cards and said, "Sign next to the X. This gives us consent to treat you today."

I handed her back the pen and signed paper. "Do you have a restroom I can use?"

"Down the hall. Have a seat in the waiting room when you're done." She pointed across the hall to an empty room with a TV playing the morning news.

The dark-haired, beautiful Karissa walked into the room. "How are you?"

"I'd be better if this was over and I had cancer-free results." Grabbing my purse from the chair, I followed her to a dressing room.

Karissa handed me a key to a locker and two hospital gowns. "Take your shirt and bra off and put on these hospital gowns. It's the same as last time. The first should open in the front and the second in the back."

"Why do they make me wear two?"

"Because you'll walk down hallways where people can see you, and they want to make sure you're covered." Karissa smiled at me, which put me a little at ease. "After you dress, bring the key and sit on that chair." She pointed across the hall to a plastic chair in a room with only a curtain for a door. Then she exited the room, closing the door behind her.

I waited my turn in the chair, not looking forward to the needle's prick. Finally, a technician entered the room and put on rubber gloves.

I said, "Last time, saline leaked out under my skin, causing it to get puffy, so can you put the IV in my left arm?"

"OK. Your vein probably burst." She looked at my arm, trying to spot a good vein.

"I didn't realize veins could burst." I watched as she tied my arm with the rubber strap.

She tapped on my arm, looking for the best vein to use. "Yes, they can. Or the catheter could've dislodged a little."

After she finished, Karissa greeted me and escorted me to the monster I needed to face. "Climb up on the steps and take off your outer gown. Just so you know, when Dr. Wolfel starts the biopsy, it will sound like a loud drill. So don't be afraid, and try not to jerk when you hear it."

The other technician pulled my gown aside as I stretched my arms over my head and inserted my breasts into the openings facing the floor. At least this time, all my weight wasn't resting on my sternum. My weight was evenly distributed between my stomach, above my belly button, and my head. That was great since I'd had terrible chest pain for days after my last MRI experience.

"I'm going to tighten compression plates around your left breast so it doesn't move during the procedure." Karissa tightened the machine while the other technician inserted earplugs and headphones over my ears.

"Are you ready?"

Hesitantly, I said that I was. Oh, how I longed for this to be over. My bed moved as they pushed me into the machine, but my eyes remained closed just as they had been when I climbed the steps while holding onto Karrisa. I didn't want to see the beast that filled my nightmares. I kept telling myself I could do this as the clanking, clicking, and humming noises started. My arms were cramped in a matter of minutes because they were awkwardly positioned above my head—time for a distraction. I thought about where I'd got to with the poem I'd started the last time I faced my demons.

'Twas the night before Christmas; I
longed for the past,

When my family was whole and my joy
still held fast.

The stockings were hung by the chimney
with care,

But I ached for my son, who was no
longer there.

I nestled with Mike in the warmth of our
bed,

While a vision of heaven danced round
in my head.

I soared up above, through the clouds,
and took flight,

And I know I met Jesus in heaven that
night.

A high wall of jasper, a huge pearly gate;

My eyes opened wide when I saw my
son's fate;

Luke's home, now eternal, beyond all
my dreams,

God's peace and the throne where his
holy light beams.

An ocean of crystal and lanterns of gold,

A rainbow of emerald; such sights to be-
hold!

The thunder, the lightning, the fanfares
galore.

Such wonders I'd never imagined before.

Karissa interrupted my work. "Tammy, we're going to insert the contrast
into your arm. You'll feel it burn for about ten seconds. OK?"

I assumed she meant the dye. I didn't answer her since my face was buried
in the hole in the table. She probably knew it was OK; I'm sure it was just
protocol for her to tell me. After the burning finally subsided, my heart
started racing. Since I'd had issues last time, I really should have asked about
the side effects before I let them do that again. But I hadn't. Hopefully, I
wouldn't die. Trying not to think about it, I continued working on the poem
as the machine whirred.

The Bible tells more of this wonderful
place

Where all Christians go when they finish
their race.

If you turn to Jesus, he'll open the door,

To a home up in heaven with riches in
store.

Bang. The whirring and clicking of the machine stopped, and I was pulled
out. "Stay still, Tammy. Dr. Wolfel is looking at the results from the scans.
Then she'll be with you," a voice said.

Several minutes passed. "Tammy, this is Dr. Wolfel. I've located the lump
using the images from the MRI." An icy hand touched my breast. "I'm
cleaning the area with soap. That's what you feel."

"OK."

"I'm going to administer the numbing agent so you don't feel the needle
when I do the biopsy. You'll feel a small pinch before the lidocaine enters,
but you should be numb in a few seconds."

The pinch hurt, but I kept my mouth shut as I felt a stinging sensation.

"Your breast may feel cold, but that's OK." The doctor said something to
the technician, but I couldn't hear her through my earplugs with headphones
over them. "I'm going to insert the needle to do the biopsy. If you feel any
pain, please tell me immediately, and I'll stop. I don't want to hurt you."

"I understand."

"If it hurts, we can administer more lidocaine." She inserted the needle, and it sounded like a drill. As it went deeper into my breast, I felt
mild discomfort. Click. Click. Buzz. Then it started hurting more, but not
enough that I told her to stop. I just wanted the procedure over with, and I
didn't want to risk having to come back to get another biopsy or, worst-case
scenario, a false positive, or false negative result. So I gritted my teeth and

powered through as I finished my poem and thought of Luke's peaceful, pain-free life in heaven.

Luke's presence was with me. God's love
filled my soul,

And I knew all my problems were under
control.

The sadness I felt about losing my son,

Has now turned to joy, for his pain is all
done.

My son is at peace, and for certain, I
know,

My vision was real, but my life's down
below.

"I'm almost finished," Dr. Wolfel said. "Just hang on a little longer, Tammy. You're doing great." It felt like a jackhammer going in and out of my breast with the sound of a drill as they continued to gather several samples out of the suspicious lump with a vacuum-assisted device. Needing to get my mind off the pain that I was sure would kill me, I thought of my son and the visit with him in my poem as I finished writing it in my mind.

I came back to earth where there's still
much to do,

I'll finish the race, then I'll join my son
too.

My visit to heaven had caught me off
guard,

I thought of the murder and how I'd
been scarred.

But if I trust God and I share my faith
story,

I'll help other people discover his glory.

So what did I learn from the death of my
son?

A new life awaits us when this one is
done.

Hold on to your faith and keep up the
good fight,

Merry Christmas to all, and to all, a good
night.

After the procedure, I had to go into the machine one last time to make
sure everything had gone as planned. When I came out of the machine,
Karissa removed the clamp that had held my breast. Immediately, I felt pain
as my breast hung through the hole. I don't think the pain was coming from
the incision site; I suppose it came from the pressure of the clamp squeezing
me too tight.

"Tammy, Dr. Wolfel is here to talk to you," Karissa said.

"Hi, Tammy. You tolerated the procedure well, and there weren't any
complications. Pathology will send your results to Dr. Stefanick in three to
five days."

Pushing up on my arms, I looked into Dr. Wolfel's big brown eyes.
"Thanks."

"This will be the last time you see me. It was nice meeting you."

"Thanks, Doc. I hope never to see you again too." We both laughed,
understanding the hidden meaning and hope that I wouldn't have any future
problems.

13. Not Following Instructions

A marker had been placed in my breast to show the location of the biopsy, so it was necessary to get a mammogram. This is done after all biopsies, and the marker won't set off the metal detectors at the airport when you go through security, or so I was told.

An older lady with blond and gray hair led me to the machine, where she told me to stand straight. She placed a clear plastic compressor around my breast and walked behind a glass partition. "Hold your breath." The machine hummed for a few seconds. Then I heard a beep before the technician said, "OK. You can breathe."

For the following image, I stood sideways, and she tested my abilities as if I were auditioning to become a contortionist. "Put your arm across the machine and rest it here," she said, touching the back of the white machine. "Then, lean your body back."

I almost fell over as she pushed me into position, and I was glad I only had to hold the pose for a few seconds. Next, she said, "Keep your belly facing the machine, but turn your upper torso to the wall on the right." I did as she instructed, and she compressed my breast once again. It was painful where it wasn't numb. Either that or the local anesthetic had already worn off. I had a hard time holding my breath for those few seconds. My lung capacity had been getting worse over the years, and ten seconds were my limit. I was free to go after a quick three-image mammogram to ensure the marker had stayed in position.

"Here's an ice pack for pain," Karissa said as she escorted me through the maze to the dressing room so I could dress and gather my belongings. "It was great seeing you again." She left to head to her next patient.

I carefully dressed and shoved the baggy with the tiny ice pack and paper into my purse. Since I was on a diet, I'd run out of fruit, so a quick stop at Walmart was needed, even though I was still somewhat dizzy. My heart felt like it would explode, which was probably the dye since I had felt that way the last time too.

· ♥ · ♥ · ♥ · ♥ · ♥ ·

While shopping, I got so lightheaded that I didn't think I could drive home, so I bought a bottle of cherry Pepsi and ate a Payday. After loading my groceries into the car along with the puzzles I'd bought Mike as a Valentine's Day gift, I sat in the driver's seat of my Lexus and contemplated if I could drive. I was so tired that I considered taking a nap. But I didn't exactly feel safe doing that since there had been robberies recently, so I started the car and listened to music on the way home.

· ♥ · ♥ · ♥ · ♥ · ♥ ·

Depressed about the possibility of having cancer, I cheated on my diet and ate an entire order of breadsticks from Fox's Pizza. Then I texted Mike, Mom, Jamie, and a few friends who had been praying for me.

> The biopsy was very painful, but I'm glad it's over. We're leaving the country on Saturday to visit Turks and Caicos for one week. The results are supposed to take three to five days. I hope I get them before the trip because I don't know how often I'll have reception outside the country.

After Mom exercised in our gym in the basement, she came upstairs to talk. As I was speaking, I bumped my breast. "Ouch!" After that, I was in dire pain for the rest of the day. When Mike came home, I hugged him tightly. "That was awful. It hurts so bad. I hope the pain goes away before our trip."

While we finished packing, Mike walked into the bedroom carrying the plastic bag Karissa had given me. "What's this?"

"It's an ice pack Karissa gave me."

"There's a paper in the bag with the ice." Mike held up the paper. "It has discharge instructions on it."

"Oh. I didn't know. What's it say?"

"For the first twenty-four hours, apply a cold pack over your dressing to reduce swelling and bruising." Mike took the minuscule two-by-three-inch ice pack and put it in the freezer. "It says to repeat every hour as needed."

"Oh boy." Grabbing the paper from him, I said, "I hope I didn't lengthen the time I take to heal since twelve hours have already passed since my appointment."

The other instructions said to watch for bright redness, swelling, drainage, or heat at the biopsy site, so I made a mental note in case of a reaction. Since the ice pack had taken thirty minutes to freeze, I only had time to use it twice before bed.

·♥·♥·♥·♥·♥·

The next morning, I thought about skipping my shower and leaving my dressing on for an extra day. But it would have been my son's twenty-fifth birthday if he'd still been alive, and I'd found a few friends I'd known from when I'd worked in real estate to meet at a sixty-minute prison break escape room in Richland, so that was out of the question. I was terrified to remove the bandage, even after I'd iced it twice.

Our adventure in the escape room was fun. The attendant split us into two groups, one in each of the two cells. But I couldn't do some necessary things to solve the clues, like putting both my arms through the jail bars to unlock the combination lock. The lock was too far, and I had to push my breast on the bars to reach it. Kyle had trouble getting his arms through, even after removing his jacket. His mom was the only one with arms thin enough to do it. She tried but couldn't unlock it, even though we had the correct code. Thank goodness the attendant finally came in and unlocked it for us because time was ticking.

My friend Fran and my husband were in the other cell, and we both got out together to proceed to the following clues. Fran was a pro and zipped through the next portion while we all shouted the numbers she needed to unlock the obstacle. In the third room, Fran again took first place for getting the most clues, but Mike and I did OK, and Kyle and his mom were having a blast. We all had so much fun. Ultimately, as with the other escape room, we were two clues away from breaking out of prison. Maybe next time. And there would be a next time because we all agreed to do another one soon.

·♥·♥·♥·♥·♥·

Two days later, I got an email from Conemaugh Hospital that read, "You have a new message in Conemaugh My Chart! Please sign in to read your message." I immediately logged into the website to see if it was the biopsy results. An addendum read, "Pathology results demonstrate fibroadenoma to a nodule. Pathology results are concordant with imaging findings. The remaining sonographic findings can be followed in six months for stability. Routine screening mammogram should be considered." Assuming I was cancer-free, I emailed and texted all of my prayer warriors. At least I could relax on my trip the following day. I wasn't sure about what the future would hold with me getting more mammograms, but I know they can be beneficial for almost everyone and can save lives if cancer is found right away. But with my tender lumps, the pain was unbearable, so time will tell if I can ever get another one. I'm not a doctor, nor do I want to give medical advice, but I know my own body and how much pain I can bear.

·♥·♥·♥·♥·♥·

The bandage that was supposed to fall off in a few days never did. It was probably because I was careful not to get it wet, bump, or rub it whenever I scrubbed myself in the shower. I removed it myself on day eight. The area was still slightly bruised and sore. I couldn't wait for it to heal.

My phone hadn't rung the entire week we were on vacation while Mike and I enjoyed gorgeous sunsets and relaxed, listening to the sound of the ocean as it lapped onto the beach. But life had returned to normal in snowy Pennsylvania, so I called my doctor. Jill answered. "Hi, Jill. I got my results from My Chart about ten days ago, and I just wanted to follow up and see if Dr. Stefanick needed to see me for anything. I've been out of the country for the last week."

"OK. Let me pull your chart. What's your date of birth?" After giving Jill my birthdate, she put me on hold. The phone clicked a few minutes later when she reconnected the call. "Tammy, the pathology came back, and everything is benign, but Dr. Stefanick didn't leave me a note. She'll be in tomorrow. Can I call you then?" She confirmed my telephone number and hung up.

At least the secretary had confirmed that I didn't have cancer. Imagine if I'd misunderstood the diagnosis. That would have been a nightmare. But all was well, and God had my health in the palm of his hand. Just like he always had in the past, in the present, and in the future. Jill called the next day. The woman's indifferent voice said the doctor was happy with the results. God is good—all the time. I needed to trust him the next time I had a health scare, and I'm glad he was always with me and cared for me, even when I had doubts. Never for a moment did I think he *couldn't* control the situation, but I didn't know his will and if he would let me face my trial by having to fight a battle with cancer. I'm glad he chose not to make me suffer, and I hoped I could move past the pain from the mammogram that felt like it would kill me so that I'd get another in the future. It's better than finding cancer too late and having to get radiation because that would terrify me. Everyone needs to choose what treatments they need for themselves since it's their body. Most people would disagree with my decision about not getting mammograms, and they are probably correct. But I'm a baby when it comes to pain.

If you have a health scare, remember that God has everything under control and surrender your life to his skillful hands. Then look for specialists. And if you disagree with their opinion, get a second and third opinion if necessary. Do whatever you need to so that you feel comfortable with the outcome. When I needed a biopsy, I didn't trust the first doctor who had suggested it that first year when they had found a suspicious lump. But when she again told me I needed a biopsy one year later, I sought a doctor I'd seen in the past who I respected. She was the one who sent me for the biopsy after holding my hand and telling me how important that procedure was. She even hugged me before I left her office.

At my biopsy appointment, I met an intelligent radiologist who said she needed an MRI to see if a problem existed since the images on the ultrasound weren't clear enough to warrant a biopsy. God put all the right people in my path to care for me. And I didn't even know it then. I looked at the doctor's online profiles and checked their education, ratings, and how many years they'd done their job. Then, I decided if I agreed with their suggestions. It was my life; only I could choose how to live it best.

My advice is the same for my readers who aren't Christians. Never let the troubles of this world or your life cause you to worry, because that will do more harm than good. You only have one body. So live life the best you can, and if you need to start over, it's never too late to change how you live so you, too, can have a new life.

14. FEAR OVERRULED LOVE

One month before my trip to Australia, I panicked. I texted Nate.

> Will you go to Australia with me as friends?

As soon as I hit send, I knew I'd made a mistake. I'd been thinking about sending that text for over a month. But every time I typed the message into my phone and was about to hit send, I backspaced over it because I'd changed my mind. There was a battle inside me.

Two demons and one angel argued.

Demon One said, "Go with Nate. Sleep with him and have the trip of your life."

Demon Two argued, "You can hang out as friends and have a fabulous time. You don't have to sleep with him. Men and women can hang out together for days without developing feelings for each other. And even if you do develop feelings, there's no need to act on them. Unless you want to. But whatever you do, it's OK because it's your life, and you're the boss."

The Angel said, "You know what God would want you to do. God doesn't want you to think about being with anyone other than your husband—friends or not. The Bible is clear. You know it is. And you know what's right. I don't need to argue my case with you because I see the tears rolling off your chin. Those tears wouldn't be there if you thought it was OK to cheat on your husband. When you married Mike, you became one in God's eyes; as Matthew 19:5 says, 'For this reason a man will leave his father and mother and be united to his wife, and the two will become one flesh.'"

Part of me didn't want Nathan to say yes. But another part of me wanted him to because I feared going halfway around the world alone. In fact, I was terrified. Now I was waiting to see what he would say. I wanted to be a faithful wife. I genuinely love Mike with my whole heart, and I didn't want to lose him or the perfect life we had. We complete each other sentences. We like the same food and mostly enjoy the same travel plans.

But lately, I've also fantasized about Nathan and me sightseeing in beautiful Australia on this once-in-a-lifetime trip where I'd walk into the hotel, and he'd hug me, lifting me off my feet and swinging me around before giving me a huge bouquet. Then he'd kiss me like no one had ever kissed me before. He'd grab my hand, and we'd run through the hall to our room. Candlelight would lead the way to the balcony, where we would drink champagne and eat under the starry sky as he made a toast to my beauty. The tears that had once filled my eyes would no longer be there because he'd say he was deeply in love with me, and his wife had divorced him, and I'd know my body belonged to him and him alone.

Why wouldn't Mike go with me? Why wouldn't he sit on a plane that long? Mike is perfect! But he's not, because he won't travel. How long would it take for Nate to answer me? I saw us walking arm in arm, touring the rainforest, the Sydney Opera House, the outback, and so much more. But I couldn't see us in bed. My mind wouldn't go there because I loved Mike so much.

Nate finally replied.

> I won't be able to keep my hands off you!

OK. I should have expected that. I didn't know what to say.
Nate texted again.

> Will you be able to keep your hands off me?

I replied.

> I can't honestly answer that.

I knew the answer to his question, but I would never tell him or anyone that I'd once fantasized about taking him out of the friend zone.

·♥·♥·♥·♥·♥·

One night in the outback of Australia, I went on a sunset tour, and the group celebrated with a bottle of wine. Well, let's just say I celebrated alone. The tour operator set the bottle out, and no one but me was drinking it. So I got drunk because I was trying to get my money's worth for the $133 I paid for the tour to watch a big rock turn orangish-red. Yes, I know it was a stupid idea. I've also learned that I should never drink wine when I'm alone because it makes me sink into a deep depression. Wine and I don't get along.

After watching the sunset at Uluru, I returned to my hotel; I called Mike and scared him because it was early morning. He thought something had happened to me. After I assured him I was fine, I let him go back to sleep. Then I texted Nate a music video because I was too embarrassed to tell him how I felt. It would become too real if I typed the words, but I felt less guilty sending the video. The words were obvious.

Or at least they were to me.

You can have me.

All of me if you'll tell me you love me.

Even though I know you don't and can't
love me.

He couldn't because he had a wife. The music in my text said more.

Give me what I need.

Only for one night.

I knew what I meant—I wanted his love. That new feeling you get when you first fall in love with someone and they make you feel like the queen of the world. But he would never provide me with that love. Or could he? Those words probably make little sense, but I cannot quote song lyrics. So you get the gist of it.

He replied.

> My wife doesn't like intimacy.

Did that mean there was hope?
But his subsequent text left me in shock.

> So I can only have you for one night?

I replied.

> For as long as we have.

What had I just done? I couldn't believe I'd done it. I'd offered to cheat on Mike. But why?

15. A Journey of Faith, Forgiveness, and Self-Discovery

As I reflect on the terrifying journey that led me to this moment, I can't help but be overwhelmed by the weight of my own choices and the grace that carried me through. It all started with a simple message from Dr. David Jeremiah that said not to worry, but to put my faith in Jesus instead. Little did I know that those words from Matthew 28:18 would become a lifeline, guiding me through the darkest corridors of my soul.

Each twist and turn, every obstacle, has shaped me into the person I am now. The journey has been turbulent, marked by loss, heartache, a health scare, and a relentless pursuit of lust that started with an indecent proposal.

God wanted me to trust him. But I hadn't listened. My faith was in *me*, not God, who knew all things. Temptation lurked within the shadows; a text beckoned me toward the cliff of self-destruction. When Satan saw I was attracted to a gorgeous man who tried to knock me to my knees, I found myself trapped in the tangled web of my own desires for a new life—a life where I felt loved, adored, and needed.

Mike didn't love me any less than he had at our wedding. He constantly told me he loved me, even though I weighed almost two hundred pounds. But something was wrong if I wanted to have an affair with a handsome man who lusted after me. I teetered on the edge of temptation, grappling with insecurities and desires that threatened to consume me whole. It was a battle against myself—a battle I was losing until I heard the gentle whisper of God's voice, beckoning me to return to him, to surrender all I am and all I've ever been.

But could I? Sure, I could. But would I? Would I allow God and Mike to love me the way they had before my impure thoughts changed my life? Reading my Bible, praying, and surrendering control of my life back to God were the perfect ways to start. Only then could I get my life back. The life I hadn't realized I'd had all along.

·♥·♥·♥·♥·♥·

So what happened with Nate? Absolutely nothing. He texted.

> Let's just stay friends.

He was no longer our doctor because he'd moved to another office further from where we lived. I focused on listening to the Holy Spirit living inside me, telling me not to betray my husband. Even though Nathan was as handsome as ever, the more I looked at his picture, the less alluring he became and the less I thought about him. I guess I was looking for the feeling you have when you first fall in love with someone. I didn't want to be with someone else; I just wanted the feeling that came with a new relationship. But whatever had caused me to think of cheating and sinning by having those impure thoughts, God healed me and removed Satan's hold on me because I again surrendered my life to Jesus, just like I had when I became a Christian at the age of thirteen. I also remembered a lesson I'd learned many years ago: a woman and man shouldn't be alone together for long periods because that can lead to temptation. So I'm glad we hadn't tried to take the trip as friends because that could have ended in disaster for both of us.

And you know what else? I'm glad God permitted me to be tempted because I'm realizing again how blessed I am to be loved by a wonderful, God-fearing man like Mike. I discovered a newfound strength—an unwavering resolve to resist temptation and embrace the life that had always been mine for the taking. And something else lingered in the back of my mind. I truly believed that God would have and maybe did protect me from breaking my marriage vows because I'd been praying every morning that he would protect Mike and me from evil and anything we did that went against his will for our lives. He definitely wouldn't want me to cheat on Mike.

I'm filled with a sense of gratitude for the blessings that surround me, for the love that sustains me, and for the hope that propels me forward. So there I was at the finishing line—the starting line for my new life. I took comfort in knowing that I wasn't alone—that with every step I took, God walked beside me, guiding me with faith as my compass, forgiveness as my guide, and self-discovery as my destination. Three steps forward into my new life and two steps back into my old life were still one step ahead into the life I'd always dreamed of. The life I had all along.

Besides that, do you remember when I said it takes two to tango? During a lengthy conversation, I realized Mike strongly desired to spend quality time with me. When I asked why he didn't, he said, "You're writing on your laptop for twelve hours every day. How am I supposed to spend time with you?" With that discovery, I learned to prioritize what meant the most to me—Mike, his presence filling every corner of my heart. All those years, I had convinced myself that I was unworthy of love, but at that moment, everything changed. Mike's inability to show me his love rested solely on me, and I couldn't escape that truth. So I forgave myself for my mistakes and vowed to do better.

Do you also wrestle with the demons of self-doubt and insecurity? Do you find yourself adrift amidst the commotion of life's storms? Maybe you also have moments when you feel unworthy of love. Like me, you need to look deep inside yourself and remember that God chose to make you. So that alone makes you worthy of love. And even if you don't believe in God, consider all the positive things in your life. Make a list of all the blessings you have and all the people you have helped throughout your life. You'll be surprised how long that list is—I know I was. We all have talents we can use to help others when they struggle. Find people who need your help, then offer your services. They will love you for your generosity, and you will love yourself because you will make a difference in someone's life. I genuinely believe that we are blessed so we can bless others.

But I still had one more thing to do to make my life right with God and with Mike. I needed to tell Mike the whole truth about what happened. But could I? Sure. But would I? Now that is the question, isn't it?

·♥·♥·♥·♥·♥·

Want to follow Tammy as she travels the world, finding adventure one journey at a time, visiting national parks, or seeing gorgeous beaches? Or even meeting a killer in court or prison? Click or type https://mybook.to/TammyHorvath into your internet search bar to see all books in the Journeys Through Life memoir series or to catch up with the first book:

When a police officer knocks on Tammy Horvath's door and tells her that her son has been murdered, her life is shattered. As she struggles to come to terms with his death, a voice tells her to forgive his killer. In *Gone in an Instant*, will God reveal himself and set her free in a way she could never have imagined? Or will Tammy's spirit forever remain broken by one man's deed?

·♥·♥·♥·♥·♥·

If you enjoyed *One Text Away*, please consider leaving a review to help other readers find a book they will love. You can submit a review wherever you find my book, even if you didn't buy it there. Just a few words will make a huge difference.

Just click or type the link below into your internet search bar.

Amazon review link: https://www.amazon.com/review/create-review?&asin=B0D892YPN6

Goodreads review link: https://www.goodreads.com/book/show/215544526-one-text-away

In Case You Missed It—Also by Tammy Horvath

Gone in an Instant: Losing My Son. Loving His Killer. **Book 1**

A son killed by a single bullet. A mother's heart shattered. As Tammy Horvath struggles to come to terms with her son's death, a voice tells her to forgive his killer.

With her soul tormented by the loss of her son, Tammy fights to get out of bed every day because she can't face a seemingly hopeless future. But Luke would want her to be happy. So she pushes forward and embarks on a journey, searching for peace, hope, and a chance to keep her son alive in her heart.

Will God reveal himself and set her free in a way she could never have imagined? Or will Tammy's spirit remain broken by one man's deed?

Life Begins with Travel: Facing My Fears. Finding My Smile. **Book 2**

A husband dead in a fiery crash. A son claimed by a killer's hand. Tammy Horvath doesn't think she'll ever smile again.

Strengthened by her faith, she bravely heads solo to Iceland to see the northern lights, where she climbs glaciers and ventures into caves before seizing the opportunity to travel more often.

Tammy will take you on a journey of love, laughter, and inspirational life lessons as she swims in the crystal-clear Caribbean Sea, gets stuck atop one of

Mexico's pyramids, endures a tropical storm in the Bahamas, and hikes amid Yellowstone National Park's spectacular scenery.

Will life's tragedies make Tammy cower in fear forever? Or can she embrace a world of adventure and find happiness again?

Deep Inside: Forgiving the Unforgivable. Loving the Unlovable. Book 3

A chilling behind-bars encounter with a killer unfolds. Step into the heart-wrenching world of his victim's grieving mother. Can the unforgivable be forgiven?

As Tammy Horvath grapples with the weight of depression following her profound loss, she discovers that no amount of exercise can completely mend her shattered soul. The quest for genuine healing takes a courageous turn as she confronts the murderer, unraveling the haunting mysteries behind Luke's tragic death.

Are the roots of Tammy's faith deep enough to make a difference? Or are Tammy's friends right in warning her against facing a cold-blooded killer?

Exploring Mountains and Beaches: Journeys Beyond Borders. Adventures Worth Pursuing. Book 4

What do you hold dear in life? For Tammy Horvath, it's the relentless pursuit of connecting with others, exploring new horizons alive with wonder, and seizing every moment while she checks off items on her bucket list.

As Tammy explores mountains and beaches in paradise, she's fueled by the allure of new cultures, creating memories that have made her who she is today. Throughout her island adventures to the Bahamas, Turks and Caicos, and Curacao, as well as hikes through national parks in the Canadian Rocky Mountains, surprises lurk at every turn—from navigating floods to fending off avian ambushes. Embracing the chaos, Tammy turns each misadventure into a story worth telling.

Join Tammy on this journey beyond borders, where each step brings her closer to the beauty of life.

***One Text Away: A Doctor's Indecent Proposal.* Book 5**

In this true story, Tammy Horvath faces an indecent proposal from a respected younger doctor while she grapples with an unrelated daunting health scare: a breast lump that grows larger, demanding immediate action. Tammy must confront her deepest fears and let faith be her compass, forgiveness her guide, and self-discovery her destination.

Will the doctor's enticing compliments threaten Tammy's resolve to remain a faithful wife, causing her to destroy her marriage? Or will she have enough self-control to resist Adonis's charm?

Click or type https://mybook.to/TammyHorvath into your internet search bar, then choose a book to purchase an eBook, paperback, or audiobook of any book in the series recorded by Tammy Horvath. All books are available on Kindle Unlimited.

Note to the Reader

About the Author

Author and speaker Tammy Horvath was born and raised on a floodplain in western Pennsylvania, where she currently resides with her amazing husband Michael. She has three wonderful adult stepchildren, along with her only child Luke, who is now in heaven with his Creator and finally at peace.

Tammy has almost three decades of administrative experience in real estate and insurance. She has volunteered for more than a decade with a Christian nonprofit providing education and other essential needs for at-risk children around the world. She has been a spokesperson for the nonprofit's needs, served in church ministries, and is always available to share her story and God's message of love and forgiveness.

Tammy and her husband still live in the same house where they raised Luke, even though she cries every time she enters his room.

Tammy will never stop grieving the loss of her only son Luke to a murderer's bullet. But she lives and writes with the assurance that she will see him again and that God will ultimately use her son's death for good. She loves sharing treasured memories of her son with anyone who will listen.

Tammy has written five books in the Journeys Through Life memoir series:

Remember that one person who hurt you, the one you can't forgive? In her first book, ***Gone in an Instant***, Tammy tells the heartbreaking story of losing her son to a murderer's bullet and the road she traveled to forgive his killer. Being vulnerable about her past and her mistakes helps readers start to explore their own. The last few chapters reveal a pathway to overcome failures and find freedom, just like Tammy did. It took time, but recently, she's been visiting Tyrone in prison. As a perfectionist, Tammy refuses to give up on anyone—even a murderer.

How do you attempt to escape what has caused you the most pain? Despite thump-in-the-stomach-harrowing challenges, Tammy's second book, *Life Begins with Travel*, reveals how embarking on a courageous journey to new destinations can cultivate emotional healing. Travel became the coping mechanism that she needed. Conquering her fears as she shares the smells, the tastes, the bumps and bruises acquired on her travels changed her and helped keep Tammy from getting stuck on the top of pyramids as she did in Mexico. The one irreconcilable truth from these stories is that travel is always transformational.

How do you navigate the suffocating weight of depression that follows a life-changing loss? A coroner's knock on Tammy's door changes her life forever. In her third book, *Deep Inside*, she tries to escape the pain through exercise. But to experience genuine healing, she must summon the courage to face the man who murdered Luke to unravel the haunting mysteries behind her son's tragic death. But only if she can pass the prison's high-tech security protocols. Are Tammy's friends right in warning her against facing a cold-blooded killer?

Do you have a bucket list that involves travel? Tammy loves to seize the moment and live life to the full by immersing herself in new cultures, feeling the warm sand between her toes on stunning beaches, and marveling at the grandeur of the Canadian Rockies' majestic mountains. Join Tammy on this thrilling journey where chaos awaits, and each misadventure unfolds into unforgettable tales in her fourth book, *Exploring Mountains and Beaches*.

Have you ever been tempted to have an affair? When a breast lump grows exponentially in one year, the doctor demands a biopsy. While dealing with stress, Tammy wrestles with the demons of insecurity when a handsome young doctor tries to sweep her off her feet. Like an addicted gambler, she considers putting it all in and betting on the win to satisfy her lust. Prepare to be captivated as Tammy navigates the shadows of doubt, trying to emerge into the light of hope in *One Text Away*, book five in the Journeys Through Life series.

Ultimately, Tammy writes and speaks so that every reader may know God's immeasurable love and that forgiveness is the essence of God's love. She can't wait for the day she meets God face-to-face and is reunited with her son and other loved ones in heaven.

Click or type https://mybook.to/TammyHorvath into your internet search bar, then choose a book to purchase an eBook, paperback, or audiobook of any book in the series recorded by Tammy Horvath. All books are available on Kindle Unlimited.

Chat with the author and other memoir authors and readers by joining the friendly, fun Facebook group We Love Memoirs at https://www.facebook.com/groups/welovememoirs/.

www.ingramcontent.com/pod-product-compliance
Lightning Source LLC
Chambersburg PA
CBHW032049040426
42449CB00007B/1040